Endorsements

"Candice has an amazing talent of sharing her heart through the poetry written in this collection. Not only does scripture just pour from her mouth but it also comes to life in these readings. From hard rhymes to soft rhymes, each line paints a beautiful picture that draws you in to our Lord and Savior, Jesus Christ. Whether you start your day or end your day, these poems will bless you with inspiration from above."

—Brek Lancaster
Fulldose Music Ltd.
Grapevine, TX

"Candice is a miracle. She was not supposed to live after five brain surgeries. God had a purpose for her. God gave her the ability to write. Candice is an author. What an amazing God! This book will inspire you to get up and do what God has called you to do. So proud of my sister."

—Robin Sonnier
singer, songwriter and worship leader
Lumberton, Texas

"If inspiration could be defined as a single one of God's creations, if the sun could be lit from a single being's smile, if sincerity could be felt through a single being's eyes, if comfort could be wrapped around you from a single being's words.....and yet all of these gifts having endured through such personal tragedy, that one single being would be Candice; she is beyond the testament of the beauty faith can bestow upon a person. What a heartfelt joy it is to find a book written by such a person with all of these qualities, for the words and pages in this book shall certainly have special meaning to each who reads it."

—Jeff Striplin
Water Utilities Manager Servant Leadership
Merit, Texas

"Candice is a survivor. Her writings express strong tones of overcoming obstacles and persevering through incredible difficulties. Candice's poetry finds a way to bring hope and encouragement even in the midst of hardship. May it bring you joy as well as you read them."

—Teresa Rogers
RealIssuesRealJesus.com
Royse City, Texas

"My sister Candice has a tenacious faith that will move you to believe God for the impossible to see His manifestation of power in your life! If you need a friend you will feel like you have one as you sit and enjoy a quiet time with Candice and her biblical poetry, stories of faith, and prayer in action. She loves speaking God's Word and living it."

—Lynda Noble
singer, songwriter, recording artist, lover of Jesus
Revivalist for end times
Last Call Ministries
Aubrey, Texas

"In her second poetry book, Candice brings more poems that are deeply moving and full of warmth. Her drive to serve God and her overwhelming positive energy project through her words. Every poem in this book is absolutely uplifting, full of peace, love, and hope. Reading this book feels like diving into a pool of encouragement; you can't help but feel blessed. Thank you, Candice, for putting your words to paper and sharing them."

—Ari Yallon
General Manager
RX7.COM
Garland, Texas

More of God's Great Love, Sent Down from Above

Delving Deeper into God's Lavishing Love

by Candice Jannise

RECEIVING FREEDOM
MINISTRIES

RECEIVING ✝ FREEDOM MINISTRIES

ISBN: 978-0-578-58188-0

Jannise, Candice.

More of God's Great Love, Sent Down from Above / Candice Jannise

First printing November 2019

Printed in the United States of America

Introduction

Do you know the magnificent Creator God loves you? The rhyming lines in this book are included to equip you with the powerful truth about His love for you, which He demonstrated by the shed blood of Jesus. When His blood is applied to your life, it will free you from your **every** sin.

The cross on the front cover represents God's love for us, and why Jesus had to die. He is God's sinless Son who paid for everyone's sins. We allow His payment to be applied to our sin, the moment we are born again.

Our salvation takes place by our belief in Jesus, by confessing Him as our Lord, and by believing He rose up after He died. The good news is all about God's love for us, and how His love was manifest through His Son Jesus. He paid for the sins committed by you and me, to set everyone who believes in Him, free!

The rainbow on the cover is to remind you of God's promise not to flood the earth again, and to pique your curiosity about His promises.

The dove under each poem represents God's Holy Spirit.
Do you desire to know more? Do you *really* want to hear it?

Before Jesus departed He said the Father would send the comforter, who would guide believers in His truth and show us things that will occur.

I chose to put the symbol of the Holy Spirit under my poems to hold them up, but above the referenced scriptures because they require no assistance. The scriptures at the bottom of the poems will further enhance your study of God's Word and give you a greater insight into the verses than the poems can fully express.

The "Authoritative Poems" are written to show how Christians should use our God-given authority, to overcome all of the works of Satan and his principalities. By delving deeper into God's Word, we will find many answers to life's difficult questions.

I pray your undivided attention being focused on God will give you more knowledge about God and a greater revelation about the depths of His sacrificial love for you!

We, us, our, you, and believers, all refer to obedient Christians.

Candice

Acknowledgments

First of all, I thank God for His love, goodness, mercy, grace, His Son, and for all of the great and wonderful things He has done!

Susan Harring, thank you for not only being an outstanding Graphic Designer but also for helping with the high-resolution interior files and the formatting help when needed. Thank you for the picture you found for the cover and the amazing work you did to make the whole cover look great!

Mary Bodine, I enjoyed the time we had walking around the park together as you captured many outstanding author pictures and the painted message on the wall that says:

"God so loved...you."

Derrick Farris, showing me how to edit the text in Word format helped me once again, son. Thank you for all of your help, including your suggestions and comments.

Kym Johns at **www.alacartesolutions.net**, I appreciate the amazing website you created, which is allowing this book to be shared all over the world!

Special thanks to my sisters, Sherry Mecom, Lynda Noble, Donna Pace, Tammy Rogers, and Robin Sonnier, brother-in-law Carl Noble, niece-in-law Natalie Hill, my high school French and English teacher Marilyn Martin, and to all my friends who encouraged me in this poetry journey: Sandy Bodeman, Jerry Caspell, Laura Gilley, Brek Lancaster, Tyo Lancaster, Martha Lange, Kenny Maguire, and Jeff Striplin. Thank all of you for your feedback.

I am genuinely grateful to my family and friends for your prayers and support that gave me the courage and strength to write these messages from God, as He spoke them to me.

Contents

✝

Dedication

I dedicate this work of love to every person who is seeking God because
of a genuine desire to know Him more.

Foreword

I have written hundreds of poems in my life, inspired by deep feelings, emotions, and experiences this world brings. But my most profound thoughts come from wonderful people who cross my path. Candice is one of those who has ignited a poetic fire within me. Her poetry is a reflection of her life. In fact, her entire life seems to rhyme with the highest purposes of the Lord. You will find enjoyment in her words, but most of all, an excitement and growing faith, as you get to know her better!

"Miracle Lady"

I met a nice lady named Candice
She's a Bible-quoting machine
Smiling the first time I met her
Being joyful is just her routine

She walked with a limp, yet no cane
So determined is she that's for sure
Five surgeries messed with her brain
Don't cross her or you won't endure

They said she would not walk again
And likely she would die
In her soul, she got mad as a hen
The Lord had a different reply

I've a plan for you, get up and walk
Learn My Word, fill your heart with My Truth
Let it flow from your mouth when you talk
I do miracles; you are the proof

Miracle Lady © Jerry Caspell
Author of two poetry books & an original music CD
Allen, Texas

In Remembrance

In loving memory of my mother, Ruth Madeline MacKay Jannise. Although she departed many years ago, I still feel she deserves to be remembered.

I also want to acknowledge my father, Cleveland Joseph Jannise, Jr. He was still here when I began writing these poems, but he passed away before I finished them for this book.

In remembrance of my dear friend, John Little, who taught me many biblical lessons, just as a Christian dad would.

Golden Nuggets from God's Word

✝

"A Genuine Prayer"

God, I don't want to receive my healing through drugs as others do;
I want to receive ALL my needs supernaturally, straight from You.

My desire is for the visible manifestations to give You the glory,
while I tell other people about Your goodness, as I share my story.

You are great, beautiful, generous, loving, AND immensely kind;
I want unbelievers to know this, so they will have a change of mind.

God, will You please help me overcome all of my unbelief today?
I hope to share You with others who will believe what I must say.

I genuinely pray for every evil-doer to repent, to never be the same,
after they hear of Your salvation offer, obtained only in Jesus' name!

**Psalms 95:3; Psalms 103:3; Psalms 145:7-9, 14;
Acts 3:16; Acts 4:12 & Hebrews 10:17**

"Answers Are in God's Word"

Thank You, Father, for giving me Your words to share
with lost and hurting people who need You, everywhere.

I have found many powerful promises in Your Holy book;
To find the instructions it contains, I must FIRST take a look.

I have discovered whenever I search from Genesis to Revelation,
my hopes are raised, and my heart is filled with great expectation.

Your promises are true, so EVERYTHING You said WILL manifest;
Soon, the bad things are removed from us, and we only get Your BEST.

Your Words make me victorious when I use them to unlock the door;
Then my heart "sees" my victory, and I am NOT burdened anymore!

**Psalms 37:5; Proverbs 23:7; Isaiah 55:11; Mark 10:27;
Mark 11:23; 2 Corinthians 2:14; 1 Thessalonians 2:13;
Hebrews 4:12; Hebrews 11:1 & 1 John 4:4**

"Armor of God"

Father God, You are at my right hand, and I will NOT be moved;
Although others have often failed me, You are constantly proved.

Thank You for Your faithfulness and Your infinite mercy, Lord;
Thank You for giving me faith, and a sharp and powerful sword.

God, because of Your great love, I have all the gear I will ever need;
It was given to me through Your good, righteous, and eternal seed.

All around me, I have the helmet, breastplate, girdle, and peace,
and I can use my authority to cause my family's glorious release.

I plead Jesus' blood over myself, my children, and my siblings, too;
Thank You, God, for Jesus' shed blood; it makes us right with You.

I am thankful that, in Christ, believers have been inexplicably cleaned;
Through His precious blood, EVERY Christian HAS been redeemed!

Psalms 16:8; Galatians 5:22-23; 1 Peter 1:18-19;
Revelation 1:5 & Revelation 5:9

"Birthdays"

Birthdays are great, and they have a way of making us feel lots of love;
If today is your birthday, I hope you know you are loved by God above.

When Mary delivered Jesus, God's plan to save us was established,
and at Jesus' resurrection, God's redemption plan WAS finished.

Jesus' virgin birth was God's way of fulfilling HIS supernatural plan
of making the future right with Him and each Christian woman or man.

He had thirty-three birthdays on earth, then He died and went away,
but BEFORE His redemption was complete, He taught us how to pray.

Since Jesus is forever victorious AND He is alive once again;
When you make Him your Lord, He takes away ALL your sin.

Through Jesus, Christians and God will have everlasting peace;
Because He rose up again, the war for our souls will forever cease.

But while still here—at Christmastime—we celebrate Jesus' birth,
for our Savior healed and redeemed us, and He magnified our worth!

**Psalms 19:10; Proverbs 3:15; Luke 2:11;
2 Corinthians 5:21; Galatians 3:13;
Ephesians 2:15-16; Ephesians 4:24;
1 Peter 2:24 & Revelation 1:5**

"Blessed Is He Who Meditates"

Blessed is the one who does not live by the instructions of the ungodly,
but walks in the Father's love with joy, integrity, and faith, so uprightly.

Throughout the day and all in the night, on God's Word, he meditates;
He will sit like a tree, be still, and on his Savior, he patiently waits.

I am a child of God who has chosen to stay connected to the Vine;
Therefore, I am now partaking of this life-giving, brand-new wine.

The one who studies God's Word becomes quite prosperous;
He will receive the BEST from the Lord—and NOTHING less.

When one of God's obedient children asks anything in Jesus' name,
the Father grants the request as He would for His Son, just the same.

Everything a follower of Christ Jesus does will produce good fruit,
and he is showered with prosperity in life because the Son is his root.

If you desire the blessing and favor of God to forever abide with you,
ask the Lord Jesus to come into your heart—and only HIM pursue!

**Genesis 12:3; Joshua 1:8; Job 36:11; Psalms 1:1-3;
Psalms 25:13; Psalms 27:14; Matthew 13:23;
John 14:14; John 15:5; Romans 15:8-12
& Revelation 3:20**

"Blessings Are on My Head"

I was created in righteousness, and I am also holy,
so God's blessings are found on the top of my head.
Today I am kept safely in Christ Jesus, my loving Savior,
but before He came into my life, I WAS unquestionably dead.

Jesus' crucifixion lets all God's children be more than conquerors;
Therefore, we should not ever think about ourselves as being defeated.
On the contrary, we must trust God's Word and remember our victory
through our Lord, Christ Jesus has already been perfectly completed.

I choose to trust the promise of triumph that I have already been given,
and similar to Jesus' Words about every trouble, I will say, "It's finished."
I won't permit the devil's wicked works to continue in my purchased life,
and I will gladly declare his plans against me ARE daily being diminished.

I choose to worship God with both of my hands lifted up quite high,
while with joyful, melodious praises to Him, I will now delightfully sing:
"Christ Jesus is my victorious, eternal Lord, who is my Savior, Healer,
Deliverer, Provider, Redeemer, and my righteous, soon-coming King!"

**Job 22:28; Proverbs 10:6, 11; Mark 11:23; John 19:30;
Romans 8:37; 2 Corinthians 2:14; Ephesians 2:5;
Ephesians 4:24; Colossians 2:15; 1 Peter 2:24
& Revelation 11:15**

"Compliments Come When We Live Right"

Jesus offended many people who lived by regulations and rules;
He respected God and taught His GOOD ways to His disciples.

I know when I'm living like Jesus and offend others, it's a compliment;
My persecutors allow me to receive from God, a unique or special present.

These treasures I receive, lift me much higher above the cultivated ground;
Up here is where the victories from the Father are continually being found.

God, I thank You for Your children You send me to teach them Your way;
I pray they will listen to ALL of Your Words I am passionately led to say.

Your righteous Words I speak to them are victorious promises from You,
and as they finally learn the truth, they will KNOW what THEY should do.

Living Jesus' way allows us to excel, even as we bless those who are rude;
Telling lost people about God's redeeming love can change their attitude.

The peace we speak puts markings on our hearts—God's Words are real;
He wanted us to be made right with Him, so us, He could save AND heal.

Our tongues write the story we live, whether good or bad, just like a pen;
This tiny, yet powerful weapon can be the key that frees us from within!

**Psalms 45:1; Proverbs 7:3; Proverbs 16:20;
Proverbs 18:21; 2 Timothy 3:12 & James 3:8**

"Determine Your Purpose"

Every day, God supernaturally blesses Christians
with amazing benefits, with quite a large load.
His unfailing mercies are new to each of us
as we walk on His beautiful, less-traveled road.

The Lord shall preserve us from ALL evil;
He will save all of our blood-bought souls,
but first, we must trust and believe Him,
and purposely fill our pre-determined roles.

God's people surely have a part to play in this life,
into which we have been divinely created or born.
We can choose Christ and fulfill our destiny, or live
our way AND allow our hearts to be viciously torn.

The final decision for the choices we are to make
is our God-given responsibility, for you and me.
Now, it's time for each of us to make up our mind
what our assignment from God is supposed to be!

**Deuteronomy 30:19; Psalms 68:19;
Psalms 121:7; Psalms 139:14;
Lamentations 3:23; Matthew 7:14-15;
1 Corinthians 6:20; Ephesians 5:17;
1 Peter 1:9 & 1 John 2:2**

"Distractions"

Who or whatever is presently bothering me
is only a distraction trying to stop God's provision.
I must believe that everything in God's Word is true
AND entirely agree with HIM in my final decision.

When I put a demand on God to meet my every need,
it will not cause the lights in heaven to go out or to dim.
I can trust in His Word, by using the faith He has given me,
and as a child, choose wholeheartedly to agree with Him.

My failure to completely trust AND rely on my God's Word
allows the devil to locate the vulnerable one he's searching for;
The devil, who is our enemy, seeks those who will let him
devour them—he walks about LIKE a lion, who does roar.

Satan's distractions are to keep our eyes off of the written Word
that is full of the Father's every magnificent plan, through Jesus.
We must choose to keep our eyes steadfast on our righteous Lord
and LET Him provide, offer protection, and thoroughly bless us.

As I think in my limited heart, undoubtedly, that is who I am.
Therefore, as a born-again child of the living God, it's in my favor
to disagree with anything that will come against the Lord or me,
and be joined as one-spirit with my victorious AND eternal Savior.

It's such a great pleasure to be a highly prized child of our God,
who wants His children to abundantly prosper and to be well.
His plans for Christians are good and NOT for our destruction,
so He sent His perfect Son, Jesus—to save believers, from hell!

**Proverbs 23:7; Jeremiah 29:11; Luke 1:37; John 3:16;
Romans 3:4; 1 Corinthians 6:17; 1 Corinthians 15:57;
Ephesians 1:7; 2 Thessalonians 3:3; Hebrews 12:2;
1 Peter 5:8 & 3 John 1:2**

"Faith Comes through Jesus"

Bible faith comes by repeatedly hearing it, NOT by having heard;
Therefore, to become victorious, we must remain in God's Word.

Jesus is the word of God who came to live with mortal man;
To redeem us from our destruction was God's chosen plan.

I am thankful that in my paid-for life, my JESUS is the center;
He gives me wisdom in what to do since He is my loving mentor.

— — — — —

Father, I thank You for giving me the encouraging words to say
to the lost and hurting people YOU chose for me to inspire today.

The truths I speak about You help them open their minds to receive
because Your Word ALWAYS works for those who TRULY believe.

I want to effectively minister about Your everlasting love for them;
My prayer is: they will receive Jesus, who is my diamond, my gem.

With Your beautiful rainbow, Your covenant with us was made;
You redeemed us through Jesus, by whom our debt was paid.

God, You have done many things for us, beyond our finding out,
so when I think about Your goodness, it makes ME want to shout!

**Genesis 9:13; Psalms 103:4; Proverbs 3:13-15;
John 1:1, 14; Romans 10:17; Romans 11:33;
1 Corinthians 1:30; 1 Thessalonians 2:13
& 1 John 2:2**

"Forever with the Lord"

I thank my Lord for His cross, for the beautiful sacrifice He did,
since it let God forgive me for my every sin, even when I was a kid.

I found as I grew older, to live right, there was a MUCH better way;
We CAN imitate Christ Jesus by walking in love with others each day.

Although I live a pure life now—perfect on earth, I will NEVER be,
and that is one reason Jesus came to earth—so He could save ME.

My spirit-man has been perfected, so from Him, I will not want to hide;
Instead of living in darkness—with my Savior, I will ALWAYS reside!

**John 3:16; John 8:32; 2 Corinthians 3:18;
2 Corinthians 5:21; Ephesians 1:7; Hebrews 10:14;
1 John 4:16-17; 1 John 5:7 & Revelation 21:3**

"Fruit of the Spirit"

I had good fruit placed into my heart when I was born anew;
Among these, I received love, joy, peace, and long-suffering, too.

I also obtained gentleness, temperance, faith, meekness, and goodness;
These gifts combined have opened my eyes and made me speechless.

I stand in awe of my Savior's grace, and how He gave me the authority,
if someone yells foul language at me, I can toss those words into the sea!

The next truth is about the power you have, with the fruit of the spirit;
I believe it is imperative for you to begin to understand, as you hear it.

Each time something goes wrong with a Christian mom's girl or boy,
she is still able to function peacefully, because of her God-given joy.

Assuredly, she can use her gift of faith, and stand up against that germ;
In her heart, she can search for God's Word, and His promise, reaffirm.

Since she knows her victorious Jesus paid for EVERY person to be well,
"In Jesus' name, get out of my son, Spirit of Infirmity!" she will boldly yell.

Soon, her little one is confident in Christ, and feels excellent once again;
With Jesus, he learned he could stand against ANY problem—and WIN!

**Matthew 8:13; Mark 11:23; Luke 10:19;
2 Corinthians 2:14; Ephesians 6:13-18
& 1 Peter 2:24**

"God Directs Us"

Thank You, Lord, for this beautiful, blessed, and outstanding day,
in which I can praise You and thank You in an enthusiastic way.

The promises You've given me have been tried and found to be true;
They tell me You are great and You have GOOD plans for me, too.

I ask You to specify Your purposes for me You have flawlessly made,
and show me the steps I must take, to get everything my Jesus has paid.

Thank You, God, for guiding me in the direction I am supposed to go,
for teaching me to reveal You to others, so You, they will also know.

I may have an idea for what I want to accomplish, in my conscious mind,
but You will reveal YOUR perfect plans, in YOUR way—ever so kind.

I trust You, Lord Jesus, more than I ever imagined I could in the past,
and I believe these feelings in my heart, for You, will ALWAYS last!

**Psalms 18:30; Proverbs 16:9; Jeremiah 29:11;
Matthew 7:7-8 & Galatians 3:13-15**

"God Hears and Answers"

Each time we ask our godly requests, God hears and answers right away;
If we don't see the answers, we know that evil spirits can be the delay.

God is faithful, so Christians can thank Him for answering—it is done;
All authority over the evil spirits was given to us by God's amazing Son.

Jesus told believers whatever we loose, or that which we bind
is bound or loosed by God; the answers come, so results we find.

The Lord Jesus completely healed every person on the cross at Calvary;
Often we must believe what we need is done, before "it" our eyes will see.

If it was provided in the atonement, we WILL have whatever we say,
when we ONLY believe God, and we may have it FROM Him today!

**Jeremiah 33:3; Daniel 9:21-23; Daniel 10:12-13;
Matthew 7:7-8; Matthew 9:29; Matthew 10:1;
Matthew 18:18; Mark 11:24; Luke 10:19; Ephesians 1:3;
1 Peter 2:22, 24; 1 John 1:2 & 1 John 5:14-15**

"God Is My Supplier, My Supply"

The constant presence of Jesus in THIS life is my continual supply;
When non-believers see the works He does, His power they can't deny.

People want miracles to occur in their own lives, as they see in mine;
They also earnestly desire an impartation, or two, from the Great Divine.

My Shepherd is using me to lead hungry people into salvation for Him;
Through God's Words I say, they are learning He HAS also freed them.

My faith stays dependent on Christ, and in Him, I am to be confident;
My assurance in God comes from His Word, in the time I have spent.

It is delightful to know, although heaven and earth will soon pass away,
God's Word will accomplish His purpose, and for us, forever WILL stay.

— — — — —

Father God, You are my Loving, Magnificent Creator, who is my supply;
Every GOOD thing I get comes from You, and this truth, I won't deny!

**Isaiah 55:11; Matthew 24:35; Philippians 4:19;
Hebrews 13:5 & James 1:17**

"God Loves You"

God's care for people goes to such an unimaginable and great extent,
He tore the veil that separated us, so He can forgive us when we repent.

God loves you so much—He knows how many hairs are on your head;
You were made for His pleasure—so He doesn't want you to stay dead.

The Almighty's love is beyond what any of us can begin to understand
how He sent His Son to free us from EVERY sin committed on this land.

He has good plans for your future—if you want to KNOW them, ask;
Since He promised to answer you, He will show you your special task.

Let's obey God's Word and keep our eyes on Jesus, and we will prosper;
To look at the winds and waves will cause us to sink, with God I concur.

When aggravation suddenly arises from the dark places down below,
the victorious power of Jesus, by my faith, I will be happy to show!

If you haven't yet received Jesus, repent at last, and don't be late;
He is returning VERY SOON—not much longer will He wait!

**Isaiah 55:9; Jeremiah 29:11; Matthew 7:7-8;
Matthew 9:29; Matthew 10:30; Matthew 14:30;
Matthew 27:51; Romans 9:17; Romans 11:17, 24;
Ephesians 3:20; 1 Thessalonians 2:13;
Revelation 4:11 & Revelation 22:20**

"God Sent Jesus"

Thank You, God, for those You send me to give hope to, for Your glory,
while letting me share You with them, through my miraculous story.

I want to teach lost people, so they will know Your written Word is true,
and tell them awesome things do happen when Your people trust You.

Having a pure and undivided heart that loves You and fulfills Your plan,
is what You desire from EVERY PERSON—boy, girl, woman, or man.

Sometimes we tend to get focused on things pertaining ONLY to this life;
Instead of our thoughts being on You, they may be on a husband or a wife.

Lord, setting our minds on carnal things is not what You taught us to do;
You want us to STAY spiritually-minded AND to keep our eyes on You.

Oh Mighty One, You are the first, as well as the triumphant last;
While we remain here, You want us to have a good time, a blast!

Father, You are the awesome Beginning and also the victorious End;
To help us cross from this life to You—the Lord Jesus, You did send!

**Deuteronomy 31:7-8; Psalms 37:5; Isaiah 44:6;
Matthew 6:26, 33; John 3:16; Romans 8:6; Romans 14:8;
Colossians 3:2; Hebrews 12:2; 1 John 4:4; 1 John 5:7;
Revelation 1:8 & Revelation 22:13**

"God's Beautiful Key"

My hands were prepared for battle, and all of my fingers trained;
I say, "The war is now over, and nothing against me has remained."

Today my soul is at peace from every battle that was against me,
and I am resting in God, far away from our defeated arch-enemy.

I am here at this moment to tell you the exceptionally good news;
When Jesus died and rose up again—the battle, Satan did lose!

My Lord promised me His sweet victory and it, to me, He gave;
Then He handed me His beautiful key, to help Him, others to save.

With the key Jesus gave me, I can bind or loose with my voice;
The things I don't want MUST FLEE—they have NO choice.

The things I call forth will surely come to me; they have to obey,
because I genuinely believe there is power in God's Words I say.

Confess Jesus as your Lord, believe He died and rose once again,
and these truths will unlock the door to God, for YOU to enter in!

**Psalms 55:18; Psalms 144:1; Matthew 16:19;
Romans 10:9; 2 Corinthians 2:14
& Colossians 2:15**

"God's Chosen Seed"

Are all of your priorities lined up as they really should be?
Do you put God's kingdom first, or are things "All about me"?

If you seek God's kingdom and position it in your life first place,
each of your needs will be added or will go into its proper space.

Child of God, you WILL have whatever you need;
This promise is given to those who are God's chosen seed.

Everything Jesus has now, God's chosen ones will also inherit,
as is written for God's children who are one, with Him, in the Spirit!

**Matthew 6:33; John 15:16; Romans 8:17;
1 Corinthians 6:17; Galatians 3:29
& Philippians 4:19**

"God's Great Love"

Everything that's wrong with me, I DEMAND you to leave now;
I bind AND command you to shrivel up and die—that's HOW.

It's been a long journey, but I declare you're here past the allowed time;
I have been forgiven, by God, for all my sin against HIM (my crime).

This moment, I command you, Spirit of Infirmity, to NOW go away;
By my authority from Jesus, you MUST obey, so victory is mine today!

I confidently declare, "By the stripes of Jesus, I am already healed;
The evidence of my God's GREAT love is currently being revealed!"

I live in a body abounding with radiant health—it is already done;
Victory is mine, through the resurrection of God's obedient Son.

— — — — —

Thank You, Lord Jesus, for completely setting this Christian free;
I am grateful to You for giving me such an incalculable victory!

**Job 22:28; Mark 11:23; Luke 10:19; John 8:36;
1 Corinthians 15:57; Ephesians 1:3, 7;
Philippians 2:8 & 1 Peter 2:24**

"God's Love for Me"

God, I ask You to help me know to a greater degree,
about Your fabulous and unconditional love for me.

Please reveal Your glory to my heart's inner eyes,
so of Your genuine love for me, I can really be wise.

As for demonic attacks, Jesus gave me authority over them;
Very soon, they will ALL bow down—in submission to Him.

Thank You, Lord Jesus, for giving me unparalleled victory,
over every predicament—because of Your true love for me!

You paid the tremendous price I owed for my every culpable sin
and freed me from hell—now heaven, one day, I WILL enter in!

**Matthew 7:7-8, 21; Luke 10:19; John 3:16;
Ephesians 1:7; Philippians 2:10-11; Colossians 2:15;
Hebrews 12:2; James 1:5 & 1 John 2:2**

"God's Protection and My Spiritual Authority"

God, it surprises me we have armed officers in our churches
for the safety of Your children—to protect each of us from harm.
However, You are the One who works to keep us safe, through them;
Therefore, Your sanctified people have NO need for any type of alarm.

Your obedient angels are constantly surrounding Your righteous
people, to keep us all safe from every sort of horrifying pain or trouble.
So when any one of Satan's monsters tries to come in and attack us,
we have the authority to cast those evil spirits away, on the DOUBLE!

Father, I thank You, because of the sinless shed blood of Christ Jesus,
I am under the New Testament, and not bound to the first, for it is old.
With this new way of victorious living You have generously provided,
You told me to resist Satan (the devil); therefore, I will be VERY bold.

Lord, You said I am to exercise my spiritual authority over demons;
I can declare to them where they are to go, and what they are to do.
When I speak confidently in Your name, my great and loving Savior,
each of the evil spirits must obey me, just as they always obey YOU.

I have been given power over serpents and scorpions—this means,
anything that will attempt to come against me can do NO sabotage.
I will bind up and cast into the sea, anything that comes my way,
and by using the authority I have been given, I WILL safely lodge!

**Psalms 34:7; Isaiah 41:10; Matthew 18:18; Mark 1:27;
Mark 11:23; Luke 9:1; Luke 10:19; Hebrews 8:13
& James 4:7**

"God's Vision"

The vision belongs to God, so mine has to die and allow His to begin;
First, I have to keep listening to my Savior, so in this life, I WILL win.

Second, I must follow Jesus' way and know, through Him, I AM able;
I have to wholeheartedly grasp my faith is real, and not a story or a fable.

For the job God has given me to do, He will provide the needed vehicle;
His work in my life will be finished with victory, in every arduous battle.

Specific duties from Jesus are available for your accomplishment, too;
The requirement is, trusting God's Word, which He has written for YOU.

From His divinely orchestrated and detailed plans, don't ever stray,
because it's extremely beneficial to LET Father God have His way!

I hope you believe these powerful words I am sharing while saying,
"If you're struggling to receive the Lord's truth, I hope you are praying."

Open the eyes of your heart to inwardly see what His plans are for you,
and His gentle tug will lead you safely down the road you are to pursue!

**Psalms 23:3; Isaiah 30:21; Jeremiah 1:12;
Jeremiah 29:11; Matthew 7:7; John 14:12;
Romans 8:28; 1 Corinthians 10:11; 1 Corinthians 15:57;
2 Corinthians 2:14; Ephesians 5:17; Philippians 1:6
& Philippians 4:13, 19**

"God's Word Is Not Void"

Almighty God, Your powerful Word will never return to You void,
and I believe this, so when there are lingering problems, I get annoyed.

Lord, I ask You for wisdom on how I am to speak and make them obey;
Therefore, everything that is amiss must heed Your powerful Words I say.

Whatever I desire, I get to stand on Your promises and plant the seed,
and then I will find I have abundantly received every good thing I need.

Then others begin to notice the bad things have gone and abandoned me,
and they begin pondering if Jesus is the one who can also set them free.

Each time I do not doubt in my heart, and I believe WHEN I pray,
blessings commence to fall, and improve my situation, right away.

The effective working power of God's Word is the total explanation;
Through MY faith, is one way I can receive the desired manifestation!

**Psalms 4:11; Psalms 85:8; Isaiah 55:11;
Mark 11:23-24; Luke 17:19; Romans 12:3;
Galatians 6:7; Philippians 4:19;
1 Thessalonians 2:13 & 1 John 5:14-15**

"Good Ways to Live"

Receive Jesus in your heart and, of His instructions, obey,
then, forever with Him and His Father, you will live each day.

Put God's kingdom before all the other things you want to do,
then everything you genuinely NEED will be given to you.

Speak peacefully AND always be exceedingly kind,
and when you make a promise, don't change your mind.

Believe Jesus arose from the dead; confess Him as your Lord, as well,
and your life after earth will be good—when here, you no longer dwell.

Each time you give, with love, to those who have a legitimate need,
the Lord will abundantly bless you for your good AND selfless seed.

Show kindness to the domestic and wild animals living all around;
The birds in the air, the fish in the water, and those in the ground.

Love each of your neighbors as MUCH as you LOVE yourself;
When you live these ways, you'll have genuine or spiritual wealth!

**Deuteronomy 1:15; Psalms 15:4; Proverbs 12:10;
Matthew 6:33; Matthew 7:21; Mark 11:23; Mark 12:30-31;
Luke 6:38, 45; Luke 10:27-28; John 3:16; Romans 10:9;
Galatians 5:16, 22-23; 1 Thessalonians 4:17; Hebrews 5:9;
James 2:8 & Revelation 21:3**

"Grow Like a Tree"

Currently, I am like a green olive tree in God's possession;
I have the ability to grow abundantly—even amid a recession.

I can plant God's seed where I work, in my home, or at the gym,
but the everlasting life anyone can get may ONLY be given by Him.

I speak good words to a person and believe God will give the growth;
However, it is evident to me that I, by myself, cannot do them both.

The righteous person shall surely sprout up like a flourishing palm tree,
and in the future, he will live in peace with God—absent from his enemy.

Without breaking—into a flattened position, these trees do easily bend;
They stay planted, since deep down in the soil, their roots, they do send.

Each time the winds cease their pelting blows, the palm trees will arise;
The same is true for those who are righteous in God's observant eyes.

For the man of God who gets knocked down will undoubtedly rise again,
because his soul is anchored in Christ, the One who forgives ALL his sin!

**Genesis 26:12; Psalms 92:12; Proverbs 24:16;
Isaiah 41:12; 1 Corinthians 3:6; 1 Corinthians 6:9-11;
1 Corinthians 15:4; Hebrews 6:19; 1 Peter 3:12
& Revelation 21:3**

"Healing"

Every illness is finished, just like my triumphant Jesus said;
Body, you WERE healed when Jesus rose up from the dead.

Your Lord HAS set you free, from sickness of every kind;
Will you believe this is true? Will you make up your mind?

The thoughts of our salvation, and forever setting mankind free,
propelled the Lord Jesus to pay the price owed for all humanity.

— — — — —

Thank You, Jesus, for Your sinless blood that washes away each sin,
which allows those who make You our Lord—heaven, to enter in.

Your blood has also removed from us every sickness and disease,
and its life-giving power sets each believer free from ALL of these!

**Matthew 4:23; Mark 16:6; John 8:36; John 19:30;
Ephesians 1:3; Colossians 2:15; 1 Peter 2:24;
2 Peter 1:3 & 1 John 2:2**

"I Am a New Creation"

The old "me" has passed away, and now my new "me" is born again;
I am eternally thankful to God for rescuing me from my every sin.

In innocence, I have meticulously washed BOTH of my hands;
As a result, I am now ready to accomplish all of HIS plans.

When I listened to what the Lord told me with His quiet voice,
the message I heard from Him caused me to GREATLY rejoice!

Lord, Your Word tells me I am born again; I have been made new,
and it also says, You have created me to be a mirror image of You!

In Christ, I am forever changed (spiritually) into a NEW creature,
and God's Spirit of truth (His anointing) is now my brilliant Teacher!

**Genesis 1:27; 1 Kings 19:12; Psalms 26:6;
Psalms 73:13; Psalms 143:10; Matthew 10:8;
John 14:16; John 16:13; 2 Corinthians 3:18;
2 Corinthians 5:17; 1 John 2:27 & 1 John 4:17**

"I Am a Real Jew"

Lord, my heart has been born again and made brand new;
It longs to obey Your Word and to humbly abide with You.

My inner man has been beautifully AND permanently changed;
As a result, I have been washed spotless and divinely re-named.

The scriptures tell me being a real Jew is a matter of my heart,
so this means I am a real Jew now, with a refreshing new start.

I did not replace the Jews by receiving Jesus' payment for my sin,
but my professed faith in Jesus let God, into His family, graft me in.

Thank You, Lord, for teaching me this GREAT news is true;
Now the real me follows wholeheartedly after the real YOU.

I know You truly love me, God, this I understand more every day;
I learn about Your love from Your Word I read, and also when I pray.

Today, I bless every blood-bought Jew who is born again in You;
Lord, my request is: You will show me what else, for You, I can do.

Please give me the wisdom to know how to accomplish Your will;
It is for Your glory that I desire to do this; it is how I genuinely feel.

You said if I lack wisdom, then I am to ask for more from You;
I trust You will give it to me, just as You said You would do.

You are exceedingly faithful, so much that no person can outdo,
and I believe ALL of Your promises will certainly come through!

**Romans 2:29; Romans 11:17; 2 Corinthians 1:20;
2 Corinthians 5:17; 2 Timothy 2:13; Hebrews 8:6;
James 1:5; 1 Peter 1:23; 1 John 4:8 & Revelation 1:5**

"I Am Chosen"

Lord, thank You for Your gracefulness, gentleness, provision, and peace,
Your love and comfort, AND away from the enemy's hand, our release.

All who live a godly life will suffer the enemy's wrath and persecution,
but when we stand on Your Word and use our authority, Satan will run.

My Savior, You are truly good and always deliver us from every trial,
even though sometimes it SEEMS to take You quite a LONG while.

God, I invite You to use me as You please, for I am Your currency;
In Your time frame is what I ask because I feel there is no urgency.

It brings great peace to my heart to know, in my spirit, I am very strong;
I have the power to kick Satan from my life, where he does not belong.

This authority was given to me by my Lord Jesus, God's beloved Son;
My obedience to Him lets Jesus call me HIS friend—I am a chosen one!

**Luke 10:19; John 1:3; John 15:14-16;
2 Timothy 3:12 & James 4:7**

"I Am Forgiven"

Because I have accepted Christ Jesus in my heart as my Lord,
after I meet Him, He WILL give me HIS promised reward.

I believe Jesus supernaturally rose again after He was dead;
I trust this miracle occurred three days later, as He formerly said.

I am forgiven by God because He forsook Jesus—God accepts me
because His only begotten Son, He alternatively condemned on the tree.

Today, I am alive and doing well because of Jesus—because of Him;
I am happy to tell this great news to others, so He can also save them.

God's Holy Spirit now dwells inside me—Oh, such liberty!
My triumphant Lord and Savior Jesus, HAS set me free!

**John 8:36; Romans 10:9, 17; 1 Corinthians 3:16;
2 Corinthians 5:18; Colossians 2:13; 1 John 2:2
& Revelation 22:12**

"I Have a New Name"

Thank You, God, for the magnificent way You saved me;
I am very grateful You have set this former captive free.

When I received Jesus, You gave me a whole new name;
Now that He is in my heart, I will not ever be the same.

The instant I made Jesus my Lord, I became a whole new me;
Spiritually, I was changed into who You created me to be.

In my soul, You are NOT finished working on me YET, now,
but in Your mercy, You will make me a better person, somehow.

I really hunger to be just like my Lord Jesus; I thirst to be like He;
I genuinely desire His amazing reflection to shine down upon me.

I want to lay hands on sick people and see them ALL recover,
and do these mighty works, to be like Jesus, my big Brother!

**Isaiah 61:6; Matthew 12:50; Mark 16:18; John 1:42;
John 8:36; 2 Corinthians 5:17; Philippians 1:6;
1 John 4:17 & Revelation 1:6**

"I Have Authority"

God, thank You for Your Son Jesus, who taught me
that using His name against Satan is my authority.

Since I have NOW bound every evil spirit against me,
I BOLDLY declare I am healed, blessed, and I can see!

Because of Jesus' stripes, I was able to resist the devil today,
so he and all of his evil spirits I bound, HAD to go away!

Lord, thank You for YOUR blood, which has set me free,
and for giving ME all power and authority over the enemy!

**Matthew 18:18; Mark 16:17; Luke 10:17-19;
John 8:36; Ephesians 1:3; Colossians 2:15;
James 4:7 & 1 Peter 2:24**

"In Christ Jesus"

I thank my God for always causing me to triumph in every adversity,
and for turning ALL the problems around, so they are a benefit to me.

I am living continually in Christ Jesus and serving my loving Lord;
He has already promised me, I will certainly be given a GREAT reward.

As long as I follow God, the godly requests I ask Him, I will receive,
for my faith allows His power to do the things, of Him, that I believe.

Each time my enemies come against me like angry flooding water,
my God will rise up against them because He is a trouble-spotter.

He is faithfully keeping me safe, with His fearless angels all around;
I can almost hear them praising God—Oh, such a glorious sound!

I am grateful He affectionately accepts each believer in Christ Jesus,
and thank Him for the eternal home He is preparing for each of us!

**Ezra 8:31; Psalms 5:12; Psalms 138:7; Isaiah 59:19;
Mark 11:24; Luke 2:13; John 3:16; John 14:2;
John 15:7; Romans 8:28; Ephesians 1:6;
Colossians 3:24; Hebrews 1:6 & Revelation 22:12**

"In God's Presence"

God, I want to live in Your presence, where there is fullness of joy,
to stay away from the devil and his every wicked scheme, or ploy.

Father, in Your righteous right hand, there are such radiant pleasures;
You have an amazing way of blessing us with Your great treasures.

Each time affliction arises against us, and there is foreseeable trouble,
You are always so duly committed to BAIL us OUT, on the double!

Father, You are great, and You will lift Your people up higher,
especially when confronted with an enemy (a thief or a liar).

Your obedient children do not have to worry or fret right now,
because You are great, and You WILL work it out, somehow!

**Psalms 16:11; Psalms 18:48; Psalms 34:19;
Proverbs 10:6; Isaiah 41:10; Isaiah 59:19;
Isaiah 61:7; Luke 1:37 & Romans 8:28**

"Into Our Neighborhood"

When the Lord Jesus came to earth, into our neighborhood,
He was specifically sent by God, for mankind's ultimate good.

The hurts, struggles, and misery, which are sent to harm us
are not from the Father God, or His Holy Son, Christ Jesus.

The devil is the evil one who steals, kills, and tries to destroy us today;
We resist him by living right and obeying God's Words, in every way.

There is no evil in our God—He is good, ALL the way through;
He's so profoundly good, His Son came and died—FOR YOU!

Everyone who submits to Jesus will escape God's future wrath;
His blood cleanses them as if they are taking a detoxifying bath.

Because He is kind, God did NOT want anyone to receive damnation,
so He appointed Christians, through Christ, to obtain eternal salvation!

**Psalms 119:68; Matthew 4:10-11; John 1:14; John 3:16;
John 10:10; John 14:12; Romans 5:9; Ephesians 1:7;
Philippians 2:8; 1 Thessalonians 5:9; Hebrews 10:10-14;
James 4:7; 2 Peter 3:9; 1 John 2:2 & Revelation 1:5**

"It Is Already Yours"

Quit trying to get what you ALREADY have, or got;
You are healed and blessed, whether you know it or not.

By the stripes of Jesus, you HAVE been healed;
Believing God's Word WILL LET IT be revealed.

I'm fighting today's battle in the stance of victory
because I know what Christ Jesus HAS done for me.

Believe in God's Word, while embracing YOUR success,
and the truth in His Word will free you from your mess.

It is the perfect time to put a smile on your beautiful face;
By faith, receive ALL of your needs, through His grace.

Confess God's Words, and believe every syllable you say,
and you WILL see what you said—even possibly TODAY!

**Matthew 9:29; Mark 11:23; John 8:32; Ephesians 1:3;
Ephesians 2:8; Philippians 4:19; 1 Thessalonians 2:13;
Hebrews 4:12 & 1 Peter 2:24**

"It's Time for a New Beginning"

It's time for Christians to get ready for a delightful new beginning,
by obtaining a renewed life with Jesus, so we can ALL start winning.

Make a bold statement, saying, "The past is now dead and buried";
Righteous one—you, to the Son of God—are now rightfully married.

This positive declaration is ONLY the sweet taste of a new beginning,
of an unaccustomed life, which will be great forever, or never-ending.

The final desired outcome, for Christians, will for ALL eternity last,
since forevermore, we will be with our Savior, whose love is steadfast.

Mercy and everlasting truth go before our gracious Father's face;
When we are with Him, He will wipe our tears away—in His place.

Also, in heaven, our joy will not ever be stolen from us anymore,
because the enemy won't interfere in our lives—as he did before!

**Nehemiah 8:10; Isaiah 54:5; Romans 7:4;
2 Corinthians 2:14; 2 Corinthians 5:17;
1 Thessalonians 4:17; Revelation 20:10
& Revelation 21:4**

"I Will Sing Praises"

To You, Almighty King, I will sing happy and victorious praise,
on this day You have made—and my melodic voice, I will raise.

I hear the harmony of Your healing music playing gently in my head,
and I know it's on the right path, with You, I am being divinely led.

Lord, in You, I choose to rest, and I forever give my complete trust,
not in other things that will soon wear out, break down, or even rust.

Those who were bound, You have spiritually made VERY wealthy;
You have thoroughly cleansed Your children, and want us all healthy.

My sadness You have removed, and now I am dancing with festive glee,
because, through my Savior's sinless blood, I have been given sweet victory!

**Psalms 5:11; Psalms 16:11; Psalms 61:8; Psalms 68:6;
Psalms 104:33; Proverbs 16:9; Isaiah 35:10;
Matthew 6:19-20; 1 Corinthians 15:57;
Ephesians 1:3 & 3 John 1:2**

"Jesus"

To the wind, Jesus spoke peace and calmed the storm, as the Lord;
He did these feats through His faith, and spoken Word (His sword).

He raised the dead, healed others, and restored the blind men's eyes;
He did mighty miracles on earth because He was, and still is, wise.

He gave authority to every believer to do the same works He did;
Anyone who believes Him can do greater miracles, EVEN a kid.

One day in the future, He will return for those who are His children,
and then we will live with Jesus, and serve Him, forever in heaven.

God's people won't ever die, be sad, or cry while we are with Him;
Jesus is our amazing light, whose brightness will NOT EVER dim!

**Matthew 9:30; Matthew 10:8; Mark 4:39; John 11:44;
John 14:12; Hebrews 8:13; Revelation 21:4, 23
& Revelation 22:5**

"Justified"

The blood of Jesus HAS justified me,
Just as if I've NEVER committed a single sin.
This reassurance I have gladly received, means,
in every predicament I encounter, I WILL win!

God presented His Word before me and said He will
always give victory to me; this even means IN every battle.
Knowing that there is ONLY one God gives me peace,
BUT this truth, makes the demons shudder, or rattle!

The cleansing blood of my Savior and Healer, Jesus,
has caused me to shine radiantly and brilliantly white.
He is my comforter and Prince, who bestows on me
tranquil dreams as I sleep soundly through the night.

Each time I keep my mind focused only on my Lord,
He will keep me in peace that is so amazingly perfect.
Anything less than the abundance He has provided for me,
I choose not to accept it in any way, but will firmly reject.

— — — — —

Jesus, You are my awesome Savior, who has thoroughly
cleansed me AND made my life altogether brand-new.
Thank You, God, for forgiving each person who repents,
and for forming us into Your image, so we can be like You!

**Genesis 9:6; Psalms 34:5; Isaiah 26:3; Acts 3:19;
Romans 5:9; 2 Corinthians 2:14; 2 Corinthians 5:17;
Philippians 3:21; James 2:19; 1 John 4:17
& Revelation 1:5**

"Know Where You Are Going"

One day when I leave this world, I know where I'll be going,
because of my Savior's love for me, He is continually showing.

It brings me great assurance and is remarkably good to know,
in the future, I will not be going down to the pit FAR below.

By God's grace, He provided the way for everyone to be free;
I cannot earn my way—I MUST believe what HE has done for me.

Through our Savior's blood and acceptance of His payment for us,
all who receive Him as Lord will live forever with our sweet Jesus.

The Lord generously paid for MORE than our sins, which we owed;
He was the ransom (payment for our life), so this news should be told.

You can also be sure where you will go when on earth you're through,
by confessing Jesus as Lord, believing He died, AND rose again for you!

**Jeremiah 16:18; Matthew 8:11; John 8:32; Romans 5:9;
Romans 10:9; 2 Corinthians 5:18; 1 Thessalonians 4:17;
1 Timothy 2:6; Hebrews 2:9 & 1 John 2:2**

"Knowledge and Wisdom"

Father, since my faith pleases You, I can have knowledge and joy today,
so I ask to receive the needed wisdom that will bring me success, I pray.

Thank You, Lord God, for hearing and answering my sincere prayer,
which allows me to tell many unbelievers about You, everywhere.

Each place You will send me, I will feel genuinely honored to go,
to share my Jesus with others, about Your amazing love He did show.

The knowledge of Jesus will help repentant people be delivered, as well,
for, by believing in AND receiving Him, they WILL escape from hell!

**Proverbs 11:9; Ecclesiastes 2:26; Ecclesiastes 10:10;
John 1:12; John 3:16; Romans 10:9-10; Hebrews 11:6
& 1 John 5:14-15**

"Lies and Flies"

God's Word is like medicine to my body, and I take "it" each day;
I am also conscientious about choosing the proper words to say.

The positive, godly declarations you also speak over me, or you
will activate God's infinite power AND let His Word come true.

The devil is watching for an opportunity to tear Christians apart,
so each of us must resist him today, by guarding our own heart.

Agreeing with Satan's negative comments and wicked lies
can stick his abominable plans to us like honey catches flies.

Just as Jesus did, speaking God's Word will MAKE the devil flee,
so resisting him likewise, in faith, will also cause him to leave ME!

**Job 22:28; Proverbs 4:20-22; Proverbs 17:22;
Proverbs 18:21; Matthew 4:7; Matthew 16:33;
Mark 11:23; James 4:7 & 1 Peter 5:8**

"Life Is the Real Deal"

This life is not a do-over or a dress rehearsal; it is the REAL deal;
Accepting Jesus as Lord lets God puts a mark on us—His seal.

From His abundant provisions, we are blessed with a bountiful load,
and His infinite mercies are new each day, as we travel on God's road.

The Lord shall keep you from ALL evil; He will preserve your soul,
but you must believe and trust Him, AND fulfill your God-given role.

Indeed, you do have a part to play in this life into which you've been born;
You can follow Jesus and fulfill your destiny, or LET yourself stay torn.

The ultimate decision that's made can only be determined by YOU,
so make up your mind to find out what God has called YOU to do.

Doing what God wants for your life will—to heaven, let you enter in;
This place is ONLY for the people who are relatives of Jesus—His kin.

To become Jesus' sister or brother, we must submit to God's will,
which is done by obeying Jesus, the One who paid our entire bill!

**Psalms 68:19; Psalms 121:7-8; Jeremiah 29:11;
Lamentations 3:23; Matthew 7:14, 21; Matthew 12:50;
Luke 8:21; John 1:14; 1 Corinthians 6:20; 1 Timothy 3:16;
Hebrews 5:9; 2 Peter 1:10; 1 John 2:2
& Revelations 9:4**

"Live Out Your Mission"

Live out the noble mission for you, God did abundantly give
and establish it so that when you are gone, it will continue to live.

Make certain the idea, help, or true comfort you will confidently bring
can be available to the next generation, including those in your offspring.

The Lord God has innumerable victories stored up precisely for you;
He has a good purpose and a plan, which He has equipped you to do.

Your role is more significant than you can reasonably dare to dream;
Unite the chosen people, knowing you may need a fairly large team.

Child of God, your pre-determined destiny HAS drawn quite near,
so enthusiastically gather yourself together, and get everything in gear.

You can ask God for His wisdom today if you need some more,
and He will teach you what to do, for He is an outstanding mentor.

God's ordained plans for you will work, as they undeniably should;
His strategic AND personalized plans for you ARE profoundly good!

**Psalms 25:12; Psalms 32:8; Isaiah 55:11; Jeremiah 29:11;
Romans 8:28-29; Ephesians 3:20; Ephesians 5:17;
2 Timothy 2:2; James 1:5; 2 Peter 1:3; 1 John 2:27
& 1 John 5:7**

"Looking into His Face"

Mama, I wish I were with you; you're in that beautiful place,
living with the Lord Jesus now, intently looking into His face.

I want to go home—there is something that exceedingly bothers;
Nonetheless, I pray not for my will to be done, but the Father's.

I'm still here today because God has great things He wants me to do;
I know I'll be in heaven one day, and I'll be with God AND with you.

But until it's time for me to go, I MUST live out our Maker's good plan;
I know I will fulfill His call because I am much more than just "a woman."

I am a spirit with eternal life, for when I received Jesus, I was born again;
This was the glorious day He graciously, forever, washed away ALL my sin!

**John 3:15-16; John 10:30; 2 Corinthians 5:8, 17; 2 Peter 1:10;
1 Thessalonians 5:23; Hebrews 10:10, 22; Revelation 1:5
& Revelation 22:4**

"Majestic Light"

Lord, I know the place You are preparing will be exceedingly bright,
and You, the skillful Creator, will FOREVER be its majestic light.

My sovereign God, You will shine forth brilliantly each glorious day,
and Your illumination will NEVER darken, nor begin to fade away.

You are currently making the places ready for Your children,
who are blessed now AND will remain free from each former sin.

Every detail concerning Your masterpiece will be strikingly ornate;
Even Your splendid street of Gold will be exceedingly GREAT.

We can't imagine just how good ALL You are making is going to be,
but to me, the best reward will be, being WITH the King of Majesty!

**Psalms 8:1; John 8:36; John 14:2; Romans 8:18;
1 Corinthians 2:9; Galatians 3:26; Hebrews 10:17;
Revelation 21:3-4, 21, 23 & Revelation 22:3**

"Meet Jesus in the Sky"

Lord, I pray for YOUR perfect will on earth to be fulfilled, at last,
for the final Gentile to come in, so that this planet would be of the past.

I pray for those You have called into Your magnificent kingdom
to no longer run away, but to You, they will enthusiastically come.

Then everyone who belongs to You will be saved from hell;
This eternal salvation from You includes ALL Israel, as well.

Lord Jesus, every Christian will meet You, up in the sky,
and we will NOT EVER again have to tell You, "Goodbye."

With You, our Lord and Savior, we will ALWAYS get to stay;
This is true because You told us You will NEVER go away!

**Joshua 1:5; Matthew 6:10; Matthew 28:20;
Romans 11:26 & 1 Thessalonians 4:16-17**

"My Father's Love"

Father God, I greatly appreciate Your everlasting love
that came to us when You sent Jesus down, from above.

I thank You, Almighty God, for this day WITH thanksgiving,
because You give me the words I write, so I can earn a living.

Thank You for the lovely flowers You made for me to smell,
and for the aromatic fragrance, they provide for me, so well.

Thank You for giving the precious gift of eternal life to us,
through the shed blood of Your Son, who is my Lord Jesus.

I am grateful to You for being faithful, righteous, and true;
Because You are so GOOD—I give my life back to YOU!

**Psalms 33:4; Psalms 100:4; Luke 12:27; John 3:16;
Ephesians 4:9; 2 Timothy 2:13; James 1:17;
1 Peter 2:24; 1 John 2:2 & 1 John 4:8**

"My Heart and Mind"

Father, I pray for my aching heart and my limited mind
to receive Your love that's so sweet and equally as kind.

Thank You for the meaningful things You have created me to do;
I will continue to assist in people's lives, by leading them to You!

Help me let You manifest Your glory and let Your power unfold,
so You may change many hearts to repent, to be brave AND bold.

Real victory from You can only begin in my heart and my mind,
and when I don't doubt Your Word, Your TRUTH is what I find!

Your righteous and Holy Word is the key required to unlock the door,
oh, why did I NOT EVER see this intelligent, godly answer before?

These truths, which are found from Genesis to Revelation,
have joyfully filled my heart with a confident expectation.

There is no time to cry about the past—for remorse, it is too late;
It's now the hour to receive my victory, so no longer will I hesitate!

**Proverbs 23:7; Matthew 9:29; 2 Corinthians 2:14
& 1 Thessalonians 2:13**

"My Worth and Value Are in Jesus"

My worth AND value—in my Lord Christ Jesus, are found;
Not in any social media can my identity, in Him, be drowned.

I am bought by the blood of Jesus—His love can't be measured;
My worth to Him is inestimable, but I am immensely treasured.

Jesus' death and resurrection paid for my sins, and set me free;
This merciful atonement took place because my God valued me.

Although the blood of my Lord Jesus bought me—paid in full,
to obey Satan, would give him the right to me—in hell, to rule.

As a born-again child of Almighty God, the apple of His eye,
I chose to obey Him, AND live—instead of Satan, AND die.

God made me into royalty—a priest, as well as a king,
and in reverent gratitude to Him—forever, I will sing!

**Exodus 19:5; Deuteronomy 30:19; Psalms 89:1;
Zechariah 2:8; John 3:16; Romans 6:16; Romans 11:17;
2 Corinthians 5:21; Hebrews 5:9; 1 John 2:2
& Revelation 1:6**

"New Year Celebration"

Christians can have a proper celebration for the exciting New Year
by choosing to consume God's WORD—instead of wine or beer.

Being drunk in the Spirit, or on God's refreshing, life-giving wine,
is how we can decide to honor our amazing God, who is so divine.

Each child of God's devout obedience to the Father's righteous Word
can be seen as foolish by some, because it, they've never really heard.

If they will believe the good news of Jesus, about the words they hear,
they'll have faith for a future celebration, in one they'll GLADLY appear!

God's Word says confessing Jesus as our Lord will keep us from going to hell,
as long as we believe in our heart that God raised Him from the grave, as well!

**John 3:16; Romans 10:9-10, 17; Ephesians 5:18;
1 Thessalonians 2:13 & Revelation 19:17**

"Not in ANYTHING Is Our God Unable"

It thoroughly blesses my faith-filled heart EVERY time
I am enthusiastically informed of a miracle or divine healing.
For I know the death that was lingering near, was Satan's way,
in that particular area in a person's treasured life, of stealing.

Through the unmatched strength of the blood of Jesus Christ,
the sick or indigent person's body or livelihood is quickly restored.
I believe each time Almighty God's power is instantly manifested,
the devil and his demons are just gob-smacked—they are floored!

———————

When we look at the problems on earth, they seem to magnify.
Still, Lord, I know when we keep our eyes focused intently on You
and forget about the other things that insist on coming against us,
all-powerful God, there is NOT ANYTHING You are unable to do.

At this particular moment, I am stopping what I am doing,
because I feel compelled to joyfully sing to You my praise.
For all the countless miracles You have performed for us,
Your thankful people will exalt, or lift You up, ALWAYS!

Our eternally Faithful, Righteous, and Loving God, clothed
in honor and majesty, is always victorious and full of might.
My proclamation is, "The devil picked the wrong one to
initiate a battle with when he chose OUR God to fight!"

**Psalms 11:7; Psalms 104:1; Daniel 2:20; Luke 1:37;
John 10:10; 1 Corinthians 2:8 & Revelation 5:9**

"Our Daily Benefits"

Good medicine is applied to your life whenever your heart is cheerful;
It takes away the gloom, doom, and all that causes one to become fearful.

Do not go anywhere when God's cloud above you keeps hanging still;
Firmly stay there until He says to go—obediently remain in His will.

The Lord loads His obedient people with tangible benefits every day;
He freely supplies our every need, in His own unique and superior way.

My dear Lord and precious Savior holds me with His right hand, alright,
and He gives me peace during the times, with others, I desire to fight.

He forever makes us extraordinarily strong in Him, in many ways;
He has promised blessings, on Christians—for ALL of our days!

The Lord desires to fill your mouth with blessings on the inside,
so allow His favor to be poured into you by opening up REAL wide.

To the obedient people who continually walk upright before Him,
God declares He will not withhold anything GOOD from them.

If you genuinely desire to be included as one of His beautiful sheep,
confess Jesus as your Lord—AND in the future, you won't weep!

**Leviticus 26:6; Numbers 9:19; 1 Chronicles 17:27;
Psalms 25:20; Psalms 46:10; Psalms 68:19;
Psalms 73:23, 26; Psalms 81:10; Psalms 84:11;
Proverbs 17:22; Isaiah 41:10; Romans 10:9-10
& Revelation 21:4**

"Overflow with Blessings"

Faithful are the loyal children of God,
who keep their Father's pleasant ways.
He will keep them delightfully satisfied
during their life, for ALL of their days.

A poor, lonely old man is much better
than a well-to-do, yet sought-out liar.
The obedient one gets undeniably blessed,
yet the other, full of deceit, will be on fire.

The wicked man shall assuredly fall by calamity,
but the child of God, who falls, will rise again.
An obedient Christian will surely get an increase,
but a wicked person shall be cast out, by his sin.

A highly devoted man or woman of Almighty God
will overflow with supernatural blessings, many.
However, the over-sleeper and the greedy man will
be poor because their property and money will flee.

The Father will give His people joy in the
morning and great peace during the night.
With friendships, laughter, love, and peace,
should EVERY Christian genuinely delight!

**Psalms 30:5; Psalms 37:4; Psalms 127:2;
Proverbs 11:24; Proverbs 13:22; Proverbs 20:13;
Proverbs 24:16; Proverbs 28:22-24; Matthew 25:46;
Luke 11:28; 2 Corinthians 9:7 & Revelation 21:8**

"Peace through the Storm"

Since God does provide for the birds that fly in the air,
I know for ALL my needs, He will also lovingly take care.

I have fought long enough on this monstrous mountain;
Now it is time to go in and take my promised possession.

In peace, God has redeemed my soul from the battles against me;
He also calmed the storms, AND even the raging wind and sea.

Each time the godly desire comes to us, it is a tree of life;
Our hope is ultimately fulfilled after we cast out all strife.

— — — — —

Father God, I am ready and fully able to do Your perfect will;
Thank You for showing me I can, because Jesus paid my bill.

From You, my righteous God, I now have my heart's desire;
Your lavishing love for me does my heart, sincerely inspire!

**Deuteronomy 1:6; Psalms 37:4; Psalms 55:18;
Psalms 145:17; Proverbs 13:12; Matthew 7:21;
Matthew 10:29; John 14:2; Ephesians 4:31;
1 John 2:2; 1 John 4:8 & Revelation 21:26-27**

"Planning to Go to Heaven"

As suggested, I am not going to take drugs for depression;
I'm just planning to be ready when it's time to go to heaven.

While here, I will proclaim Jesus to as many people as I can,
to every current non-believing female AND rebellious man.

In heaven, God will wipe ALL of my former tears away,
and with my magnificent Savior, FOREVER, I will stay.

Daily in God's Holy temple, Him will I continually serve;
Instead of eternal punishment—me, my Lord will preserve.

I will extend my praises and thanks to the Lord Most High;
WITH me forever, He will tirelessly continue being nigh!

**Isaiah 40:28; Matthew 28:20; 2 Corinthians 2:14;
Philippians 4:8; Hebrews 12:2; Jude 1:24;
Revelation 7:15 & Revelation 21:4**

"Planted, Not Buried"

Since I am a child of God, I have been planted, not buried;
I will rise with joy because all my sorrows, Jesus has carried.

I put "Joy" back in my name when the former one was taken away;
Now I know why God gave "Joy" to me, on my original birthday.

Joy is part of the fruit of the Spirit given by the merciful Savior;
Then other fruit, such as love and peace, I also received much later.

There is more fruit available from God that I won't speak of right now;
You can get knowledge of it from the Bible; God will show you how.

All of the answers you are seeking ARE in God's inerrant Word,
but you must listen before you can believe what you have heard.

Christians, on earth, are sent by God, and we have a great mission;
We must tell others about God and us—about our reconciliation.

We are seeds, called to spring forth at the END—for harvest-time;
To lead others to God, they must repent or have a shift—a paradigm.

Every believer who receives Christ Jesus as his own Lord,
WILL go before Him AND receive His promised reward!

**Isaiah 53:4; Matthew 4:17; Luke 3:8-9; Acts 3:19;
Romans 10:9, 17; 2 Corinthians 5:18;
Galatians 5:22-23 & Revelation 22:12**

"Relationship in Christ"

Thanks for the four new tires You blessed me with, my loving provider,
how the payment was satisfied by my dad AND my generous brother.

Even more than this urgent need was paid in FULL by them, for me,
my Savior, Jesus Christ, paid for EVERYTHING I owed, on Calvary.

I genuinely do believe by the stripes the Lord Jesus bore, I AM free;
Therefore, I command EACH lying manifestation to leave, quickly!

JESUS paid for every sin I will commit, including the ones in the past;
He was crucified, yet rose again—now my love for Him will always last!

Since the truth and promises of God WILL forever remain the same,
ALL believers in Christ Jesus will always have victory—in His name!

Because I know who my Father is, to whom I now rightfully belong,
and I was made righteous in Christ—I will praise Him in a new song!

**Psalms 98:1; Matthew 18:18; Romans 5:1;
1 Corinthians 15:57; 2 Corinthians 2:14; Galatians 3:26;
Ephesians 4:24; Philippians 4:19; James 1:17
& 1 Peter 2:24**

"Revelation Knowledge"

Lord, I thank You for revelation knowledge,
which does not require my presence in college.

This kind of wisdom comes straight from You;
I cannot fail when I listen to what You tell me to do.

The mysteries we speak in an unknown language in the Spirit,
hold the key which unlocks the door with the answers behind it.

Thank you, God, for this new profound revelation inside my heart;
Thank You for showing me, in Jesus, I have been given a fresh start.

In this brand-new life You have been VERY generous to me, to give,
I now speak to the dry bones and command them to revive, to truly live.

I will search for Your lost sheep, the people You want ME to find;
I will tell each one to turn to You quickly; to change his or her mind.

It's required they confess You as their Lord before the last or final hour;
They need to know You will return soon for us, in Your victorious power!

**Proverbs 2:6; Ezekiel 37:4; Mark 13:26;
1 Corinthians 14:13; 2 Corinthians 5:17;
1 Thessalonians 4:17 & Revelation 22:20**

"Right with God"

Thank You, God, that I've been made right with You,
through ALL the suffering my Jesus had to go through.

It brings inexpressible comfort to my blood-purchased soul
when I think about Jesus' blood and how it made me whole.

Jesus completely and forever paid the price every person owed;
When He died on the cross, Your love for mankind vastly flowed.

God, thank You for telling us You have already set Your people free,
and for letting me share Jesus with those You want to save, through me.

Together with all the saints, as one body, we will bring You praise,
and we will thank You for making us right with You—ALWAYS!

**Psalms 30:12; 1 Corinthians 6:20;
2 Corinthians 5:21; Hebrews 9:26 & 1 Peter 2:24**

"See It in Your Heart"

Stop struggling to obtain what you already possess—child, you are blessed
because the Lord, Jesus (God's Son), you HAVE genuinely confessed.

Beloved, search the scriptures, and you will know what I say is true,
although I realize the things I am saying might be outlandishly new.

God's healing power to you He did so lovingly and generously send when
Jesus zealously died for you, and then three days later, He arose AGAIN!

With every horrendous stripe the Savior bore on His face and back,
He removed your penalty and stopped the enemy's legal right to attack.

By the wounds of Jesus, you have been blessed, and perfectly healed;
Through His afflictions for you, has God's love been FULLY revealed.

Your honorable Lord's promised victory is SURE to come through
if you completely trust in Him AND allow His promise to come true.

Receive whatever you need, in your heart first, I must say,
and then, with your eyes, you will see it, without much delay!

**Proverbs 23:7; Isaiah 53:5; Mark 10:52; Mark 11:23-24;
Mark 16:6; John 3:16; Romans 3:23-24; 1 Corinthians 15:4;
2 Corinthians 1:20; 2 Corinthians 5:21; Ephesians 1:3;
Colossians 2:15; 1 Thessalonians 2:13 & 1 Peter 2:24**

"Sink or Swim"

Our eternal destination is up to humanity—NOT up to Him,
whether, in this life, and afterward—if we sink, or if we swim.

We release God's provision by our belief, and with the words we say;
Abundant life, for each Christian, can be released by our faith today!

Thank You, God, for Your promises; all these vows of Yours are true;
Thanks for also using MY words to draw many new people unto YOU.

We, who are Yours—to our destination IN HEAVEN—are being led,
but those who live for the enemy—will go to a torturous hell, instead.

Jesus paid the price for our sins, and receiving Him changes our hearts;
The sword each Christian gets from Him quenches Satan's fiery darts!

— — — — —

Your eternal victory, or your defeat, is up to who YOU choose;
If you accept Jesus in your heart, then you, the devil WILL lose!

Without the Lord Jesus, you will go to hell, DEEP into the pit,
because your sin will make you, for heaven, completely unfit.

Receive Jesus, by confessing Him as your Lord with the words you say,
and believe God raised Him up from the dead, on His resurrection day!

Believing these facts about Jesus, and saying the truth about Him,
is the ONLY way to go to heaven, and NOT drown, BUT swim!

**Proverbs 4:18; Ezekiel 36:26; Matthew 3:12;
Matthew 13:49-50; Mark 11:23; Mark 16:6; John 1:12;
John 3:3; John 14:6; Romans 8:14; Romans 10:9, 17;
2 Corinthians 1:20; 2 Corinthians 5:17; Ephesians 6:16
& Revelation 21:8**

"Speak, and You Will Have It"

My physical human body is now finally obeying
all of the commands, in faith, I have been saying.

Formally our family was divided and heated,
but thanks to Jesus, the devil has been defeated.

To my perfect and righteous God, I have finally submitted;
Therefore, by Jesus' blood, of all my sins, I've been acquitted.

Since I chose to truly begin receiving freedom in this place,
I have won, through Jesus—and Satan has LOST every race.

My declaration today is, "I'm refraining from sin, so I am free,
for the enemy does not have the legal right even to touch me!"

**Job 22:28; Mark 11:23; John 8:36;
1 Corinthians 15:57; 2 Corinthians 2:14;
Colossians 2:15; 1 peter 2:24; 1 John 1:9;
1 John 5:18 & Revelation 20:10**

"The Lame Walk and the Blind See"

I speak life and health over me—I have been made whole;
ALL things that are not from God, I have chosen to let go.

My family is walking in agreement in a completely new way;
Our lives are knit together (in Christ), and in Him, we WILL stay.

Christians have important assignments chosen for us by our Lord;
There are demons we MUST make flee, by using our blessed sword.

We are united in Christ, and were instructed to fulfill God's will;
To watch God's mighty power at work gives me a GREAT thrill.

After seeing the lame walk and the blind obtaining their sight,
He helps me to sleep soundly through the exhilarating night.

— — — — —

Thank You, Father God, for the gift to me You so generously gave;
Through my testimony, I am equipped to help YOU, others, to save!

**Job 22:28; Psalms 127:2; Acts 5:42;
Romans 6:23; Romans 10:17; 2 Corinthians 5:18;
Ephesians 5:17; Ephesians 6:15; Philippians 2:13;
Colossians 4:17; 1 Thessalonians 4:17; James 1:17;
James 4:7 & 2 Peter 1:10**

"The Lord Reigns"

The Lord Jesus is my Banner, and today, He reigns;
Of the bondage from my enemy, Jesus broke the chains!

The Lord Jesus is always victorious, and forever He will live;
Jesus sacrificed His life for us—what MORE could He give?

It's the wall around our injured heart, which we can so firmly place,
that will keep us from God's love until we let Him, our problems, erase.

After we choose to release the past, by focusing our eyes on Him,
we will become joyful at last, and the problems will quickly dim!

**Exodus 17:15; Psalms 16:11; Psalms 68:1; Psalms 106:1;
Psalms 107:14; Proverbs 4:23; Proverbs 23:7;
Jeremiah 40:4; Luke 1:33; 1 Corinthians 15:57;
2 Corinthians 5:21; Philippians 3:12; Colossians 2:15;
Colossians 3:2; Hebrews 12:2-3 & Revelation 3:20**

"The Only Way"

In the very beginning, God's road was The Only Way,
but when man sinned, another road was paved that day.

There are two different roads to take—my Jesus is The Only Way;
To select the other road—oh, there is such a horrible price to pay!

There's a burning fire ready to take the man who chooses this way;
The blazing fire burns unquenchable flames each and every day.

There is a better way, my friend—please listen to what I say;
The way to God is through faith in Jesus; He is The Only Way!

Experiencing life with the Father—eternal life with His love
will bring Christians great comfort in heaven, with God above.

Which road will you choose? "It's too late for me," you say,
but as long as you have life, there's still time to change your way.

The Lord Jesus paid the price—but your salvation is up to you;
Sincerely invite Jesus into your heart—He will come if you do.

Confess Jesus as your Lord, AND believe He rose up again;
Repent of your rebellion, and He will wash away your sin.

He will lead you down the right road if this you allow Him to do;
Jesus will guide your every step, so you can go to the Father, too.

Decide to follow Christ Jesus—please listen to my plea;
The Lord Jesus paid the price, so YOU could be set free!

The Father is calling you now—please, listen to what I say;
The way to God is through faith in Jesus; He is The Only Way!

**Deuteronomy 30:19; Matthew 3:2; Matthew 7:13;
Matthew 13:42-50; Matthew 18:8; Matthew 24:51;
Matthew 25:13, 41, 46; John 3:16; John 6:44;
John 14:6; Acts 16:31; Ephesians 2:8; Hebrews 9:26;
2 Peter 1:10 & Revelation 1:5**

"The Pathway to Redemption"

For God's good pleasure, we were in His image wonderfully made,
but when Adam sinned—our debt, through Jesus, had to be fully paid.

Great health is mine because my Lord Jesus paid for me to be well;
His blood payment defeated the enemy AND saved me from hell.

I have been rightly crowned with glory, favor, and honor;
God blessed me with these—since, in Jesus, I am a believer.

The sinless, shed blood of Christ Jesus is the pathway to redemption;
His substitutionary atonement lets God forgive our every transgression.

Through His life-giving sacrifice, Christians are now divinely set free;
This is God's chosen way He made for us to have everlasting victory!

**Genesis 1:27; Isaiah 61:7; Matthew 7:9-11; John 3:16;
John 12:26; Romans 3:24; 2 Corinthians 2:14;
Ephesians 1:7; Ephesians 2:9; Galatians 5:22;
Colossians 2:15; Hebrews 9:22; 1 John 2:2
& Revelation 5:9**

"The Word Will Feed You"

When there's hurt welling up in your heart, and you must cry out loud,
your heavenly Father has compassion, for He hears you in the crowd.

God knows every time you are in overwhelming and unyielding pain;
He wants to remove all that ails you; He does not want it to remain.

God desires to use His Word to produce good fruit inside of you;
Put His love, joy, and peace together to make an excellent stew.

Believing His promises for your future will make you mentally strong
by feeding on His faithful Words, even focusing on them all day long.

His proven Word will feed you with health, to all of your tri-fold being;
Miracles can take place, and others won't believe what they are seeing.

It's from the seed you have sown expectantly on moist, fertile ground
that renders up to a hundredfold, which for unbelievers, can't be found.

Whatever we eat or drink, and all we do, must be done for God's glory;
We should tell other people about JESUS and His resurrection story!

**Joshua 1:9; Job 23:12; Psalms 34:17; Psalms 86:15;
Proverbs 4:22; Matthew 14:14; Mark 4:20; Mark 16:15;
1 Corinthians 10:31; Galatians 5:22; 1 Peter 2:2; 1 Peter 5:7
& 1 John 3:20**

"Think on These Things"

If you're worried about wrong stuff done to you, trials or sufferings,
instead of focusing on any of those negatives, think on these things:

Whatever you know to ONLY be true, good, right, and pure,
if you meditate on them, you WILL remain steadfast and sure.

Think about lovely things, or on matters of an excellent report;
Recall virtuous things—praise God—and Satan, you will thwart.

Pondering where your feet go will help correct decisions be set,
and this should keep you from falling headfirst into a trap or a net.

If you will choose to meditate on God's instructions EVERY day,
then you will be successful and prosperous, IF His Word, you obey.

Child of God, forgiveness from the Father is coming to you, quite near,
AND your success is commanded, as well—In fact, they are both here!

**Joshua 1:8; Psalms 1:1-3; Psalms 8:2; Psalms 141:10;
Proverbs 4:23-27; Matthew 21:16; Romans 6:16;
Romans 15:13; 1 Corinthians 10:11; Ephesians 1:3, 7;
Philippians 4:8-9 & James 4:7**

"Victory Is in Jesus"

Thank You, God, for Your glory You have filled in me on the inside;
I live in peace and refuse to allow my life, by anyone, to be mortified.

Because our triumphant victory is in our sweet, precious Savior Jesus,
we can receive the victory found ONLY in Him—He has redeemed us.

Jesus is my righteous Lord and this, I emphatically choose to declare;
He has set me free, so the devil cannot hold on to me, NOT anywhere.

God lifts me higher than my enemies, including the evil serpent;
God will raise you up, too, if you will turn to Him AND repent.

It's the right time for you to be completely made whole and set free;
If you've received Jesus as Lord, shout, "I'm forgiven!" with glee!

**Genesis 3:14; Psalms 18:48; Psalms 106:10; Psalms 107:2;
Matthew 5:12; John 8:32; John 10:29; Acts 3:19;
Romans 5:11; Romans 8:18; 1 Corinthians 15:57;
Ephesians 1:7; Ephesians 4:32 & 1 John 5:18**

"Wanting to Be Blessed"

Wanting to be blessed so that you can be a blessing is NOT wrong;
Having more than YOUR needs met is what God wanted all along.

Your abundant sufficiency allows you to give to those who lack,
AND opens up the blessing door for Father God to pay you back.

Incidentally, providing their necessities, with a genuine love for them,
will let this debt be repaid to you by God since it was a loan to Him.

When Jabez prayed to be blessed, and NOT to cause pain to others,
God heard his prayer and said he was more honorable than his brothers.

Therefore, it is not wrong to ask for more, so you can bless one in need;
In fact, God loves the person who cheerfully gives to others, INDEED!

**Genesis 12:2; 1 Chronicles 4:9-10; Psalms 34:8;
Psalms 35:27; Proverbs 19:17; Proverbs 28:27
& 2 Corinthians 9:7**

"We Are Blessed to Be a Blessing"

I am not to worry about my needs and how they will get met;
Jesus is my faithful Lord, and He's not finished with me, yet.

My bountiful provider is my benevolent heavenly Father, God;
Therefore lack is placed under my feet; it's already been shod.

The great "I Am" is my provider; He is "MORE Than Enough";
He has abundantly blessed me, so I can GIVE lots of good stuff.

God's designed plan is for His people to prosper ALL of our days;
His intentions are for our good; He wants us to triumph in many ways.

Praise the Lord! We are blessed to be a blessing, this is really true;
I love to bless others by teaching them to become "born again," too!

In Jesus' name, I ask for God's perfect will to be done in your life today,
and for you to come to know Him bountifully more, in a profound way!

**Joshua 1:8; 2 Samuel 22:39; Psalms 8:6;
Jeremiah 29:11; John 3:16; Acts 20:35;
Romans 10:9; Ephesians 1:3; Ephesians 3:20
& Philippians 1:6**

"Who Can Stand Against Us?"

With God on our side, who can stand against us?
What is the noise I am hearing? What is all the fuss?

Christ Jesus, for each Christian, had already prevailed
over the devil, when Satan, Jesus successfully derailed.

Open your eyes to see the good things the Lord has done;
Shout praises to King Jesus, for He HAS triumphantly won!

The enemy is defeated, but he's still walking around now,
although Jesus beat him in a way that only He knew how.

As a result of His achievement, my soul is quietly resting in peace,
so unto You, my victorious God, all that I am, I choose to release.

The promises the Lord God has spoken won't return to Him void;
Therefore, Satan's plans for Christians have already been destroyed.

Lord, Your EVERY steadfast promise concerning my life, is, "Yes,"
so I WILL obey Your Words and not give Satan, to me, ANY access!

**Psalms 55:18; Psalms 126:3; Proverbs 19:21;
Isaiah 55:11; Romans 8:31; 2 Corinthians 1:20;
Colossians 2:15; 1 Peter 5:8 & 1 John 5:18**

"Who Is Christ Jesus, the Son?"

Jesus is the Word, who was with the Father in the beginning,
who dwelt among us AND is our soon-coming righteous King.

He is the powerful, omnipotent, omnipresent Ruler, who beat His enemy,
and WILL valiantly rule ALL kingdoms—so the inferior kings will flee.

He is the Lord who IS fully God, yet He WAS also a man, as well;
The One whose blood redeems AND rescues each Christian, from hell.

He was conceived of the Holy Spirit by Mary, who was a teenage virgin;
Her obedience to God permits Him to save His people from our every sin.

His righteousness for our unpardonable sin WAS immediately exchanged;
Therefore, after our conversion—from God, we are no longer estranged.

Jesus is the Son, sent by the Father to give eternal life to us on the earth;
It is offered to all who believe in His death and resurrection, after His birth.

He is the Lord who paid for our salvation and for our bodies to be healed;
Our profession of Him allows us to get saved, and God's power revealed!

**Matthew 9:29; Mark 13:26; Luke 1:33; Luke 2:7, 10;
John 1:1, 14; John 3:16; Acts 17:7; Romans 10:9;
Ephesians 1:7, 13; Colossians 1:13; 1 John 2:2;
Revelation 11:15 & Revelation 22:20**

"Who Is God, the Father?"

He is the Father, the Holy Spirit, as well as the Son;
Each Christian's God is all three of these persons in one.

He is our only true source for every provision we ever receive;
His requirement for our blessing is, in His Son Jesus, we believe.

He is the ruler of all things, and in Him is where we truly live;
He made eternal life possible for us when His Son, He did give.

Have you received Jesus as your Lord? Do you know Him today?
No person the Father gives to Jesus will be cast out or turned away!

**Psalms 18:2; Psalms 47:6; Psalms 96:1; Psalms 139:1-24;
John 1:12; John 3:16; John 6:37; John 10:30; Acts 17:7, 28;
Romans 5:1; 1 Corinthians 2:10-11; 1 Corinthians 8:6;
1 Corinthians 12:7-11; Ephesians 1:7; Philippians 4:19;
Colossians 1:16; Colossians 2:15;
1 Peter 2:24 & 1 John 5:7**

"Who Is the Holy Spirit?"

Who is the Holy Spirit? He's part of God—He is in the Trinity;
After Jesus ascended to the Father, God sent His Holy Spirit to me.

Because He lives in me now and shows me what is to come, I won't fear;
He teaches me everything I need to know; therefore, He is welcome here.

In this life on earth, the Holy Spirit gives us our comfort, so satisfying,
because we are connected to Jesus; He is each Christian's righteous King.

The Holy Spirit is who raised the Lord Jesus from His atoning death,
and He gives all obedient Christians wisdom in life, in our every breath.

We are sealed in Him until our redemption day, which is so GLORIOUS,
because the Father, Son, and the Holy Spirit HAVE made us victorious!

**Isaiah 26:3; Mark 10:45; John 1:1, 14; John 16:7, 13;
Acts 17:7; Romans 8:11; 2 Corinthians 2:14;
1 John 2:2, 27; 1 John 4:10 & 1 John 5:7**

"Why Am I Here?"

What are the reasons I am here, God? Why did I have to stay?
Is there someone who needs You, one You want for me to pray?

Because I believe in Jesus, I genuinely know I will not ever die,
but until I leave this place, I must continue to laugh AND cry.

With tears in my eyes now, I search deeply into my broken heart,
while seeking earnestly for You, with hopes of a brand-new start.

I desire to see Your loving and gentle face that radiates with pure love,
which I will see in heaven, because of the sacrifice of my Savior above.

Heavenly Father, one day, You will wipe away my every single tear,
but until then, it is Your gentle touch I am yearning for, more each year.

I am looking for the day when I will meet Jesus on high in the cloud,
but here, my focus on Him will silence other voices, the soft and loud.

Nothing else on earth will matter, for only what God said will remain;
In the new place Christians will go, there will be no more death or pain!

Ecclesiastes 3:4; John 11:26; John 14:23-24;
Romans 8:37-39; 1 Thessalonians 4:17;
Hebrews 12:2-3; Revelation 21:4 & Revelation 22:4

"Why Are You Looking Down?"

Child of God, why are you looking down—feeling so blue?
You are sorely mistaken if you think your life is all about you.

Go outside of yourself and begin to help your father or mother,
or assist a stranger, neighbor, friend, sister, or little brother.

Put your focus on and your hope in God, and give Him your praise;
Your frown lines will upward go—and joy will show on those days.

Instead of feeling down, look up, since your redemption is coming soon;
Jesus will return for all Christians, so with Him, don't fail to commune.

Being in fellowship with Jesus will make you joyful and free,
and will also allow you to remain with Him, for ALL eternity!

Psalms 16:11; Psalms 22:3; Psalms 42:5;
Matthew 28:20; Luke 21:28; John 8:36
& Hebrews 11:1

John 3:16
God loves you!

Personal
Poems

✝

"Be Happy for Me"

If I should leave Earth before you do, please be happy for me,
because I will be with my loving Savior, who died on the tree.

Three days later, the instant Christ Jesus rose up once again,
is the pivotal moment He washed away each Christian's sin.

His death was such a beautiful and amazing sacrifice;
For our redemption, the Lord Jesus paid the FULL price.

Confessing Jesus as your Lord will also make you free,
and will allow you to remain with Him, for ALL eternity!

**Romans 4:25; Romans 10:9; 1 Corinthians 6:20;
Ephesians 1:7 & 1 Thessalonians 4:17**

"My Story, Plus an Invitation to Pray"

The real me is a Spirit, wonderfully made by God; He made me well,
but if you heard the doctors in 2004, they had a different story to tell.

They told my family that I had a brain bleed, a seizure, and a stroke, too;
As my body was badly shaking, my true being didn't know what to do.

Although I had the seizure and the stroke, as the physicians declared,
by the supernatural power of the living GOD, my life HAS been spared!

Today, I am set free in Christ; I am full of life and doing mighty fine;
Jesus' sinless blood keeps me connected to God—He is the Vine.

God strategically planned this victory from the beginning of the earth;
My Healer had a plan to set me free, long BEFORE my physical birth.

I am NOT the only blessed one for whom God sent His triumphant Son;
God also wants you to know Jesus as Lord, so from God, you won't run.

If you have not confessed Jesus as Your Lord yet, will you do so today?
To get saved now, pray the "Prayer of Salvation" on page 129, right away!

**Psalms 139:14; Mark 16:6; John 3:16; John 8:36;
John 15:5; Romans 3:24; Colossians 2:15;
Ephesians 1:3, 11 & 1 Peter 2:24**

"My Mom's Death"

Mama, it's fifteen years ago today since our family sadly lost you;
It's gotten easier with time, but sometimes I still feel a little blue.

I loved you, Mama, and that is the honest reason why
when I think about you, sometimes I can't help but cry.

My children are all grown now, and you have missed very much;
Megan has a job; Derrick is working and going to college, and such.

I've grown closer to God; I am genuinely one of His—a true disciple;
I study what He said in His Word, and of the meaning, I am mindful.

I hope, with our Father, you are both thoroughly enjoying my rhyme;
I am glad that I will be with the two of you, at the appointed time!

John 8:31, 35; 2 Corinthians 5:8 & 1 John 2:25

"Our Family Reunion"

We haven't had a family reunion in the last twenty years;
Oh, how we have surely missed a lot of each other's tears.

In times past, we had such a blast playing in the blazing sun;
There were horseshoes, a ring toss, AND even chances to run.

We saw mothers, brothers, sisters, cousins, uncles, and aunts;
We ate barbecue, chicken, and watermelon that stained our pants.

Those nostalgic family reunions were exceptionally good;
Maybe we are to resume getting together, as all of us should.

Mom and Dad are gone now, but we can think of them and play,
even though we don't know how long on the earth, we will stay.

Let's choose to love each other—let's be nice on Reunion Day;
Family, let's decide to obey God in this fun AND loving way!

Psalms 90:10; Mark 12:31; John 15:12; Romans 12:18;
Galatians 5:14-15 & 1 Thessalonians 4:17

"Problems Sleeping?"

Are you having problems sleeping at night?
Is it because the news is making you uptight?

Perhaps you are currently experiencing water deprivation,
the same as any wilting flower —such as a carnation.

One thing is sure—our bodies need to be properly hydrated,
so drinking enough fresh and clean water is NOT overstated.

Are you eating too much bread? It can raise your copper,
which, if it's elevated too high, CAN be a sleep stopper.

Bread, in excess, can also rob your body of the mineral zinc;
A lack of this nutrient can affect your memory, or how you think.

Nevertheless, the Lord Jesus, who gives life is our REAL bread,
He will be with ALL Christians forever, and we will be WELL fed.

Casting every care of yours on God will help you today, as well,
no matter if you are a mister or a lovely miss (a mademoiselle).

If you belong to Him, God's Word says He WILL give you sleep,
so cast your cares upon Him, then YOU, He WILL safely keep!

**Psalms 4:8; Psalms 127:2; John 6:35, 51;
1 Peter 5:7 & 1 John 2:2**

"To My Friends"

To my genuine and faithful friends—I am truly blessed to have a few;
If I leave first, don't be sad, only fulfill the great plans God has for YOU.

Thanks for the good times and the belly laughs we have; they are fun,
and for the great memories we have had, as we were burned by the sun.

Since you are close to me, you know I like the weather when it's hot,
but the place I am going WILL even be better because I was bought.

The blood of the Lamb purchased me—I am now FOREVER freed;
Jesus has taken away ALL my sins, and He meets my EVERY need.

With God, I will have no more sorrow, troubles, pain, or shame;
Jesus defeated these enemies by His blood and His GREAT name!

His sinless sacrifice paid it all; this is why—from sin—I am free;
Please receive Jesus so that you can be with Him, AND with me!

**John 1:29; John 8:36; 1 Corinthians 6:20; Ephesians 1:7;
Philippians 4:19; Colossians 2:15; 1 Thessalonians 4:17;
1 John 2:2 & Revelation 21:4**

christians have authority
in Jesus' name!

Authoritative
Poems

✝

"Devil, You Must Go"

Devil, your will in my life WON'T be done anymore;
I command you to pack up—leave—go out the door!

In the name of Jesus, I COMMAND you to go away;
Satan, I DEMAND you to listen and OBEY what I say.

I bind you and your demons, in the Lord Jesus' name,
AND my all-powerful God, in heaven, does the same.

God's Word says when I resist you that you will flee,
so once again, I emphatically INSIST you leave me!

— — — — —

Father, I loose Your Holy Spirit's power and anointing,
as I patiently wait here for Christ Jesus—my risen King!

**Matthew 18:18; Matthew 28:5-6; Acts 1:11;
Acts 17:7; 1 Thessalonians 4:16 & James 4:7**

"Get Out, Anger"

You evil, foul, obnoxious, destructive, and wicked Spirit of Anger,
in the name of Jesus, I bind up you AND your intolerable danger.

In Jesus' name, I command you right now to leave my child;
Demon, I order you to go into the abyss, DEEP into the wild.

Evil spirit, don't you think about coming back near us again;
Indeed, the Lord Jesus has permanently erased our every sin.

— — — — —

It's our new beginning, and I know we are genuinely blessed;
We are truly heaven-bound since, the Lord Jesus, we confessed.

In our loving, righteous Lord and Savior, I do firmly believe;
I genuinely know HIS victory, and I am NOW beginning to receive.

I declare God's blessing is on His obedient people—we are free,
and in the future, the Spirit of Anger won't cause us ANY misery!

Job 22:28; Psalms 9:6; Proverbs 10:6;
Matthew 18:18; Mark 11:23; Luke 10:17-19;
Luke 11:28; John 3:16; John 8:36;
1 Corinthians 15:57; Ephesians 1:3, 7;
Ephesians 4:24 & Revelation 20:10

"God's Word Is Powerful"

God's Word is more powerful than what I physically feel;
Everything His Word promises each person is VERY real.

He said He binds in heaven, the things we bind on the earth,
so to spend time in faith, binding sickness, reveals its worth.

Christians will have whatever we say, as the Lord Jesus said;
We can demand sickness to leave, and can even raise the dead.

We have the power to renounce cancer and tumors in Jesus' name,
by commanding them to leave, as Jesus Christ did—just the same.

We are able to release blessings, and can also reverse every curse,
by plucking them out by their roots—and they will NOT get worse.

By my God-given faith, I use my authority in Jesus' name, now;
I expect God's mighty power to work, as ONLY He knows how.

I bind paralysis, blindness, sickness, poverty, and each infirmity;
I command you to leave and allow every person to be set free.

Dear reader, I loose God's Holy Spirit power and anointing on you;
I pray for Him to have His way, by doing everything He wants to do.

God's strategic plans are good for YOU on this remarkable day;
Therefore, be enthusiastic about allowing Him to have HIS way!

**2 Chronicles 7:20; Job 22:28; Proverbs 18:21;
Jeremiah 29:11; Matthew 10:8; Matthew 18:18;
Mark 11:23; John 14:12 & 1 Thessalonians 2:13**

"Infirmities and Insufficiency, Go!"

Infirmities and insufficiency, I am evicting you today,
and I command ALL of you to leave me, right away!

— — — — —

I am receiving freedom in Christ the Lord, my victorious Jesus,
who came to give us all life—so I celebrate Him this Christmas.

However, after the joyous season, I won't stop praising the Lord then,
but instead—EVERY single day, I will thank Him ALL over again!

My God HAS blessed me, and He meets my current needs,
but it is up to me NOT to abort ANY of His righteous seeds.

God's desire is for His children to be well and to have prosperity;
One way we can release this power in us is by giving to charity.

Good health and prosperity can be restored or FULLY regained
by having the whole TRUTH about Jesus' crucifixion explained.

At His resurrection, Jesus paid the sin-debt, in full, for ALL humanity;
By His stripes, He saved, justified, healed, AND set Christians free!

**Proverbs 19:17; Mark 11:23; Mark 16:6, 17; John 3:16;
John 8:36; John 10:10; Romans 3:24; Romans 10:9;
1 Corinthians 13:3; 2 Corinthians 5:21; 2 Corinthians 9:7-8;
Ephesians 1:3; Philippians 4:19; 1 Thessalonians 2:13;
1 Peter 2:24; 1 John 2:2 & 3 John 1:2**

"Lack, Leave"

Lack, I bind you up and command you to go away;
I will not allow you anymore, in my presence, to stay.

Depart NOW, as FAR as the east is FROM the west;
You can't stay because God HAS given me His best.

Godly prosperity is what is currently in-store for me,
since my hand has been working for the Lord, diligently.

I bind anxiousness and each annoying thing I dread,
and place my TRUST only on God's Word, instead.

ALL of God's promises are GUARANTEED to be true,
so I say, "It is now time for MY amazing breakthrough!"

**Job 22:28; Proverbs 3:5-6; Proverbs 10:4;
Matthew 7:7-8; Matthew 18:18; Mark 11:23;
2 Corinthians 1:20 & 1 Peter 2:24**

"My Victory Is in Jesus"

Body, right now I declare you are working correctly;
In Jesus' name, you will bring glory to God, eternally.

I KNOW I have VICTORY by the blood of Jesus,
who purchased it on Calvary when He died for us.

Today, I am made whole by the stripes He bore for me,
and I will NEVER go back to the way I used to be!

I have the complete package Jesus gave to me:
Salvation, health, wholeness, AND prosperity!

— — — — —

Devil, you and your evil spirits, leave me today;
I bind you up and COMMAND you to go away!

Since I am a child of God, I am free;
In Jesus, is where I get my victory!

**Job 22:28; Luke 23:33; John 1:12;
John 8:36; 1 Corinthians 15:57;
1 Peter 2:24; 1 John 2:2 & 3 John 1:2**

"No Trespassing on God's Property"

All you lying symptoms, get off of me;
You are trespassing on God's property.

I bind you up and cast you away
and command you to leave, TODAY.

By the stripes of JESUS, I am healed;
Freedom, this way, is how God willed.

— — — — —

Father God, I invite You to have Your way in me,
as Your healing power is revealed for everyone to see.

Help me allow Your healing to come, as fast as a machine gun,
to the praise AND the glory of my Lord Jesus, Your perfect Son.

Thank You, now, Lord JESUS, for setting YOUR people free,
and in the future, thanks for dwelling with us—for ALL eternity!

**Matthew 18:18; Matthew 28:20; 1 Peter 2:24;
Revelation 7:15 & Revelation 21:3**

"No Weapon Shall Prosper"

No weapon formed can stand against me, not paralysis, poverty, or strife,
so in the name of Jesus, I command you weapons of Satan, to leave my life.

I bless my kids, my family, my friends, and all my surrounding neighbors;
I am thankful the Lord keeps all of us safe from any inevitable dangers.

Christians are continually blessed, AND to God, full of thanksgiving,
because Jesus' sacrifice will let us, forever with HIM, to keep on living.

There is a complete and matchless victory in our loving Savior's blood;
God gives us success, through Him, after something bad begins to bud.

Nothing can stand against our victorious AND powerful God, not ever,
for our beloved Lord Jesus will always be triumphant—FOREVER!

When what has been said in God's Word, we do believe,
we are truly blessed, AND from Him, we WILL receive!

**Psalms 18:48; Psalms 100:4; Psalms 121:7; Isaiah 54:17;
Matthew 17:19-20; Luke 1:45; John 3:16;
1 Corinthians 15:57; Colossians 1:13;
1 Thessalonians 2:13; 1 Thessalonians 5:18
& 2 Thessalonians 3:3**

"Only God's Plans Remain"

Each time the devil comes running, he wants everyone to be full of fear;
Child of God, when this occurs, tell him, "You have NO right to be here!

This unwanted distraction from you, in Jesus' name, I BOLDLY bind;
Jesus' blood has rendered you useless; in this, I have made up my mind.

God's Words have defeated your plans, and these truths I have spoken
are allowing me to live a blessed life because you are NOW broken!"

— — — — —

Only God's PLANS will remain—the ones He HAS ordained for us;
Forever, they will allow God's righteous children to STAY victorious!

**Job 22:28; Psalms 16:11; Isaiah 46:8-11;
Isaiah 55:11; Jeremiah 1:12; Jeremiah 29:11;
Matthew 18:18; Mark 11:23; 2 Corinthians 2:14;
Ephesians 1:3; Colossians 2:15; James 4:7;
1 Peter 1:23-25 & Revelation 21:4**

"Satan Is a Defeated Foe"

Satan, I demand you to go out of the door;
You have no right to me—as you did before.

I command you to remove your cataract, and take it away;
Devil, I enthusiastically serve your eviction notice TODAY!

I forcefully bind you up, as well as your evil Spirit of Infirmity;
By my faith in Jesus, I command both of you to LEAVE me.

You must also take any lingering problems on my body away
because Jesus healed ALL of me—on His resurrection day!

Enemy of God, you ARE a thoroughly defeated pest or foe;
With authority from Jesus, I bind AND demand you to GO!

**Matthew 18:18; Luke 10:19; Colossians 2:15;
James 4:7 & 1 Peter 2:24**

"The Power of Jesus"

Go blindness, go paralysis, go poverty, and everything I lack;
You must leave now, because these words, I won't take back.

With authority, I speak to every infirmity, blotch, and zit;
No more will I put up with you, NOT even one little bit.

I speak to all strife and anger—you too, are in imminent danger;
I come against you with power from God's Son, found in the manger.

Jesus came and paid the price that was owed for every person's sin;
It's because of His perfect life that I am TRULY healed from within.

The supernatural healing and redeeming power of Jesus is ALL over me;
His blood HAS blessed me, and FOREVER set this child of God FREE!

— — — — —

Lord, to You I lift my praise, while I thank You for Your divine blessing;
The demons believe but don't belong to You, so they ARE trembling!

**Matthew 24:13; Mark 11:23; Luke 2:16; Luke 10:19;
John 1:12; John 8:35-36; Ephesians 1:3; Hebrews 10:12;
James 2:19-20; 1 Peter 2:24 & 1 John 2:2**

Narrative Poems
about Bible Characters

✝

"Adam and Eve"

My lamp is filled with oil, so I'll wait on Jesus; He washed my sin;
My heart longs to hear, "Well done, good, faithful servant, come in."

If I should go to be with the Lord before you get the chance,
don't mourn and be sad for me, but do a little HAPPY dance.

I know that He lives, and my departure will be my graduation,
but if you don't know my Savior, you need further explanation.

God loved Adam and breathed into him the God-kind of life;
It wasn't good for him to be alone, so of his rib, God made a wife.

His Creator told him what tree NOT to eat of AND what trees he could;
Of all these, he could eat, except the one with an insight of evil and good.

The tree they were not to eat from, the one which God did forbid,
was the one Adam and Eve ate of, and then, from God, they hid.

God gave them the option to obey Him or to deliberately sin,
because He wanted us to CHOOSE to be with Him, in heaven.

As a result of Adam and Eve's sin, everyone was destined to hell,
but God sent Jesus, so WITH Him forever, Christians WILL dwell!

**Genesis 2:17-22; Genesis 3:6-8; Matthew 25:4, 23;
John 3:16; Romans 5:17; 2 Corinthians 5:21;
1 Thessalonians 4:17 & Revelation 1:5**

"Apostle Paul"

The apostle Paul was known as Saul until after he regained his sight;
He was blinded when the Lord came to him in a VERY bright light.

Jesus said to Saul something such as, "Why are you persecuting me?"
His response was similar to, "You are the Lord; this, I now see!"

Paul soon knew God intimately, and he remained strong,
even while being persecuted or sorely beaten, all day long.

For the furtherance of the gospel was Paul's sought-out mission;
To lead others to Christ so they could go to heaven, was his intention.

He praised God, even though each of his hands was in a stock,
because his focus was on the Lord Jesus, who was his solid Rock.

God was bigger to Paul than either his happiness or success,
so when he had trouble—God delivered him from his mess.

Paul said, "To live, it was to honor Christ, but to die it was gain";
However, he knew that for the people's benefit, he was to remain.

He lived even after a venomous snake bit him on the hand;
Then soon after, many people were healed all across the land.

Aprons or handkerchiefs were brought, from him to the sick,
which made the demons leave them, so they got well really quick!

One man fell out of a window from the third floor and was dead,
but Paul raised him, and then the man ate some nutritious bread.

We have authority from God to help the sick fully recover;
Christians are to do this in faith and act like Jesus, our Brother!

**Matthew 12:50; Mark 16:18; John 14:12; Acts 16:24;
Acts 19:12; Acts 20:9-11; Acts 22:7; Acts 28:3
& Philippians 1:21**

"Children of Israel"

Moses had a word from God; it was for Pharaoh to let His children go,
but it was after ten plagues before Pharaoh knew he couldn't say, "No."

God made all the circumstances work out FOR His people's benefit;
The Egyptians gave them silver, gold, and ALL their needs were met.

The whole group of people complained about their lack of food,
and because their water was also gone, it put them in a bad mood.

God still came through for His people, despite their unbelief in Him;
He dropped quail from the sea all around the camp—just for them.

They walked through the sea with walls of water on their left and right,
and in this water, their enemies drowned when it was no longer night.

It was when the sun rose up that they were no longer enslaved;
From the hands of their enemies, they were FINALLY saved!

We are told, "In the morning time is when our joy will come to us,"
BUT it is before this (when we believe) that we become victorious!

**Exodus 12:36; Exodus 14:27, 29-30; Exodus 15:4, 10;
Numbers 11:31; Psalms 30:5; Proverbs 23:7;
Matthew 9:29 & Mark 11:23**

"Elijah, and the Boy Who Was Raised to Life"

The widow lady who was from Zarephath heard from her
Almighty God; He told her what she was to do, one day.
He said she was to provide for a man sent by Him;
Soon, he would assuredly be coming her way.

They met when she was out picking up sticks for herself and her son
so that she would have everything she needed to prepare their last meal.
However, Elijah said something similar to, "Prepare a cake for me first,
and then God will also provide enough for both of you; here's the deal:

The promise from God is: you will not run out of your supply of flour,
and the oil required to sustain you, without a doubt, will not run dry.
God will provide for your household during the drought—because
you are giving your last portion of food to me, is the reason why."

Sometime later, the woman's young child became extremely sick,
to the point he had no more breath in him—which means he died.
The boy's mother mistakenly thought losing him was due to her sin,
so she went to Elijah, to ask him the reason; this is what she cried.

"Give up your son to me," spoke Elijah, the prophet, the man of God,
then he took the boy upstairs and immediately laid him on the bed.
To God, Elijah pleaded for the lad's life, stretched himself over him,
and prayed three times for the Lord to raise the boy from the dead.

Elijah asked the Lord to let the soul of the boy go back into him,
and when He heard Elijah's prayer, He made the young man revive.
Elijah took the lad down the stairs and brought him to the house of
the woman and said something such as, "See, your son IS alive!"

1 Kings 17:9-23

"Father Abraham"

When Abraham went his way, he produced Ishmael;
When we do something our way, we do the same, as well.

God promised Abraham he would have a baby with Sarah, his wife,
but his urgency for a baby caused him, with another, to create a life.

Ismael was born to Sarah's handmaid, whose name was Hagar,
but after their tension escalated, she took her son away, really far.

Abraham partly told about Sarah, when he said she was his sister,
but God told Abimelech the whole truth; Abraham was her mister.

Eventually, through Sarah—Isaac, the promised baby was born;
When God said to kill him, Abraham knew he would NOT mourn.

In hope, Abraham believed the words to him, God formerly said;
He doubted NOT, for he knew God would raise Isaac from the dead.

God promised to give him more descendants than the stars in the sky;
Abraham is our father by our faith in Jesus, when HIM, we don't deny.

Abraham's faith lets God bless everyone who also has faith in Jesus today;
Those who believe in Jesus know to get to our God, He is The Only Way!

Now I am blessed to be a blessing, like my righteous father Abraham;
For ALL eternity, in heaven—with him, EVERY Christian will jam.

— — — — — —

God, we will extend to You thanks and praises continually,
AND to You, Your righteous people will sing—joyfully!

**Genesis 12:3; Genesis 20:2-3, 17; Genesis 22:2, 17;
Psalms 18:49; Psalms 79:13; John 14:6; Romans 4:18-21
& Galatians 3:26, 29**

"Four in the Fire"

When the three men of God would not to Nebuchadnezzar's gods,
worship AND exalt any of them—by falling or bowing down,
the king became so mad that he instructed the people in his army to
increase the fiery flames seven times higher, for making him frown.

The order was decreed: the men were, with their hats and coats,
to be bound up tightly and thrown deep into the over-heated fire.
The flames slew the men who followed orders to throw them in,
but Jesus protected the men of God, so they did NOT expire.

Then four men were walking unharmed in the burning flames,
but the angry king only commanded his men to throw in three.
Then he emphatically said the fourth man looked like the Son
of God, and he KNEW their God was the One who set them free.

Shadrach, Meshach, and Abednego walked in the midst of flames
and out of the furnace, without the scent of fire on their clothes.
These divine interventions greatly impressed King Nebuchadnezzar,
so he converted himself, since their mighty God, he instantly chose.

Our heavenly Father loves His people, and He is no respecter of any,
so each of us should fully trust He will take care of our needs, too.
He said we are to call on Him for help in any area when necessary;
This is how we can receive OUR own supernatural breakthrough!

**Psalms 50:15; Psalms 107:6, 28; Daniel 3:15-29;
John 3:16; Acts 10:34 & Philippians 4:19**

"Joseph"

He was loved more than they; it was known by his coat of many colors,
so Joseph was thrown into an EMPTY pit, by his envious BIG brothers.

This happened when he was young; he was seventeen years old,
and eventually to Potiphar is where this innocent boy was sold.

He was good-looking in the eyes of a married, yet deceitful female,
whose lies landed Joseph in prison, AND yet, he STILL did well.

While there, two servants had dreams which came true, as he said;
In three days, the butler was restored—and the baker, hanging dead.

The Lord was with him—as a result, he became a successful man,
so when he put his hand to something, the Lord's blessing began.

He was a great leader in Egypt, after he interpreted Pharaoh's dreams;
God put him high in command—despite all others' wicked schemes.

His brothers came to him to buy grain for their family to have bread,
but unbeknown to them, it was to Joseph they were divinely being led.

They thought Joseph would kill them, as they understood he should;
He said they meant to do evil to him, but God meant it for their good!

**Genesis 37:2, 3, 11, 31, 36; Genesis 39:2, 5, 23;
Genesis 40:22 & Genesis 50:20**

"Moses"

He was raised by Pharaoh's daughter; she became the mom of Moses;
Even though he was a humble man, his life was NOT a bed of roses.

One day he killed an Egyptian, AND promptly hid the man in the sand;
Then, his fear of Pharaoh caused him to quickly FLEE from the land.

He escaped to Midian and helped some sisters draw water for the flock,
and then in the burning bush, he met God, who later became his Rock.

Moses was chosen to bring God's children to their promised place,
but every time he spoke to God, Moses didn't look into His face.

He was sent by God to help the children of Israel find their way home;
For many years, through the wilderness, the grumpy people did moan.

Although God supernaturally saved them from their many foes,
His presence did not stop them from complaining about their woes.

In his vehement anger, Moses hit the rock, but "Speak to it" was spoken;
The Israelites angered him again, so all the commandments were broken.

Moses threw the commandments down when he saw the people's sin,
because the idol they created caused him to rage, DEEP from within.

Our loving heavenly Father did many miraculous wonders through him;
Even in his old age, Moses was strong, and his eyesight was NOT dim!

Exodus 2:9,12, 15-16; Exodus 3:6, 14, 22;
Exodus 32:19; Numbers 20:8, 11;
Deuteronomy 34:7 & Hebrews 11:27

"Noah"

God set His brightly colored rainbow of promise in the cloud,
as a sign of His covenant between Him and the earth, so loud.

God told Noah He would not destroy the whole earth with a flood again;
His prior grief caused Him to drown all the other people for their every sin.

He told Noah to build an ark of gopherwood, for him and his family to go inside;
God also sent at least two animals of every kind, so the door HAD to be wide.

There were horses, cows, sheep, deer, goats, cats, dogs, lions, rams, fish,
and many other interesting animals you may like to have seen. Do you wish?

For one hundred fifty days, the waters were too deep, so they stayed in the ark;
I wonder if the animals made lots of noises AND if the dogs would often bark.

Noah sent a dove to find out if the flooded land was dry once again outside;
He knew it was almost time to go because of the leaf in its mouth, on the inside.

Once again, so Noah would know when it was dry again outside on the ground,
he sent the dove and knew they would soon go when it didn't come back around.

Noah left the ark with his wife, their sons, and their three daughters-in-law,
and until they bore children, they were the ONLY people each other saw!

Genesis 6:6; Genesis 7:15, 24 & Genesis 9:11, 13

"Rahab"

Rahab was a harlot, who God would redeem from her sin one day,
but first, two godly men needed to hide, so she hid them, right away.

As a result of her honorable act of faith for both of the godly men,
her family was saved from instant death—ALL of her closest kin.

The righteous men told her, "In the window tie up a scarlet rope";
It was to keep her family alive—their promise gave her much hope.

She is listed in the genealogy of Jesus in the first chapter of Matthew;
Jesus came to redeem believers—have you let Him redeem YOU?

By her genuine faith in Almighty God, Rahab was justified,
Despite the fact, to the king of Jericho, she previously lied.

Rahab declared the Israelite's Lord was THE Lord—as well,
and she was saved (by God) from eternal damnation, in hell!

**Leviticus 19:11; Joshua 2:1, 4-6; Joshua 2:4, 9, 11-24;
Joshua 6:12-25; Romans 3:24-26; Romans 3:23;
Romans 6:23; Colossians 1:13-14 & Hebrews 11:31**

"Samson and Delilah"

Samson and Delilah were a UNIQUE duo; they were quite a pair;
When she learned why he was strong, she had a servant cut his hair.

Because the Philistines wanted revenge, they sought to afflict him;
They desired to hurt Samson because of the trouble he caused them.

Therefore, Delilah disturbed him daily until he was extremely vexed;
Finally, when she was told the TRUTH, this is what happened next:

Because Delilah was very greedy and she was in love with money,
she conspired against him, so the men put out the eyes of her honey.

Soon his hair grew, and he killed more men at his death than in his life;
All of these events occurred because of the betrayal of his cunning wife.

No one should place the entire blame on the woman for ALL of this,
for the Lord left Samson because of sin, so the fault was equally his.

Although the Lord did depart from Samson because of his evil way,
He did answer Samson's prayer for revenge, on his final human day!

Judges 16:5, 16, 20, 21, 30

"Zacharias"

Zacharias was a righteous priest, ordained to burn incense on the day
when he heard the prophetic words the angel of the Lord had to convey.

He did not believe Elizabeth would become pregnant, as he was told,
so he informed the angel: To have a baby, he and his wife were too old.

Because of his unbelief in God's Word, his mouth was shut up tight;
Until John was born AND named, Zacharias could not utter his delight.

Zacharias prophesied that his son John would prepare the Lord's ways,
and his words were true because John fulfilled his call for MANY days!

Psalms 61:8; Luke 1:5-18-20-33-45-75 & Luke 2:14

It's all about Jesus!

Salvation Information

✝

"Salvation"

Salvation demands that the Lord Jesus, to you, becomes very real;
Believe in AND acknowledge Him, so you, He can save AND heal.

Our deliverance can only be received by God's amazing grace;
By our OWN works, is NOT how we can make it to His place.

Since God loved the world, He offered, for us, His only begotten Son;
Each person who believes in Jesus gets saved because of all HE has done.

The payment has been paid in FULL for every person's unrighteous sin;
What we must do is simply confess Jesus as our Lord, to enter heaven.

In our hearts, we must also believe God raised Jesus up from the grave;
Our belief and confession of Him as Lord allows our God, us, to save!

**Matthew 10:32; Luke 6:23; John 3:16; John 14:27;
Romans 10:9-10; 2 Corinthians 2:14; 2 Corinthians 5:21;
Ephesians 2:8 & 1 John 2:2**

"Prayer of Salvation"

If you do not know the Lord as your eternal Savior this day,
you will be God's child when you believe and repeat what I say:

"Dear Jesus, I believe You are God's ONLY begotten Son;
There is only one way to the Father—Lord, You are the One!

I believe You died for me, and three days later, You rose up again,
so I invite You into my heart and ask You to forgive ALL my sin.

Thank You for cleansing me, Jesus, for making me spotless and new;
I am a new creation, and accepted (by God) because I believe in YOU!"

**Matthew 3:2; John 1:12; John 14:6; Acts 16:31;
Romans 10:9; 2 Corinthians 5:17; Galatians 3:26;
Ephesians 1:6-7; 1 John 4:17 & Revelation 1:5**

Congratulations on your new life in Christ if you just received Jesus
as your Lord! To learn more, find a Christian church that teaches
that Jesus is the only way to the Father!

Jesus' atoning death would not have happened if there was another
way for our forgiveness (Matthew 26:39).

Also Available!

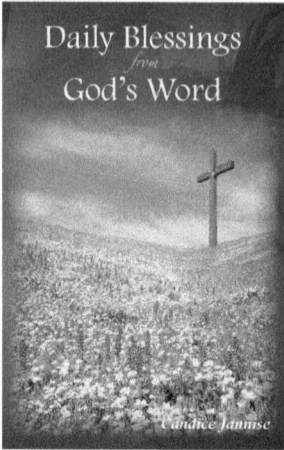

"Daily Blessings from God's Word" has three to five quoted scriptures for every day of the year quoted in a fun way! The Bible chapter number is matched to the month number, and the Bible verse is matched to the day. Each quote has an inspirational or teaching comment that follows. Some thoughts occasionally rhyme.

"Candice" is the autobiography of a Christian woman who grew up in China, Texas. As an adult, she survived a brain aneurysm, a blood transfusion, a seizure, five brain surgeries, and a paralyzing stroke. Although three times, the doctors said she would not live, Candice is still here today to tell you about God's genuine love. Her miracle story will give you hope and help you trust God for your needs.

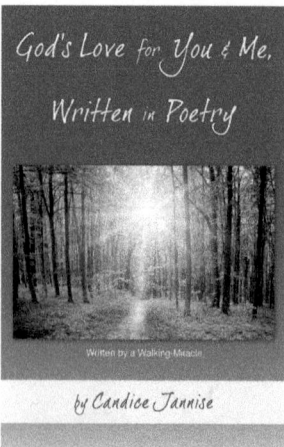

"God's Love for You & Me, Written in Poetry" is an inspirational Christian book that will bring hope and encouragement to you. The intent is to help you stay focused on God, as His Word instructs us to do!

About the Author

Born and raised in Texas, I am the tenth child, the eighth daughter of Cleveland and Ruth Jannise. I have seven sisters, three brothers, and many nieces and nephews, but most importantly, I have two grown children.

On October 28, 2004, a chiropractic adjustment caused me to have a brain aneurysm. When the doctors put a piece of metal (called a coil) in the blood vessel in my brain to stop it from leaking, my blood vessel ruptured and caused a stroke, which paralyzed the left side of my body. Details of my miraculous survival and recovery can be seen at:

www.receivingfreedom.com

Although the doctors said I would not live before each of the first three brain surgeries—after my cognitive ability returned, I wrote my first book, "Daily Blessings from God's Word".

Most of the poems I have written were given to me after I had five brain surgeries. More specifically, after I obeyed God to change churches, for unknown reasons. Within the first three months at the new church, I wrote more than one hundred Christian poems for the glory of God.

These poems began after I heard the first rhymes in my head! Then, as my loving Creator prompted me, I wrote whatever He said!

God also gave me a song I named "Jesus Broke the Chains"; it is sung by my sister, Robin Sonnier, on her gospel CD, "Come As You Are". This uplifting CD is on my website's "Shop" page.

Child of God, remember, your Father loves you, no matter what you have done because, by His grace, He freed you from His wrath by the death of His Son!

"To the Readers"

To everyone who enjoys reading the words I wrote,
I send my blessings with this final teaching note.

If you genuinely desire to live life fresh and free,
obeying and trusting God will save you much misery.

The Lord God's pre-ordained plans for you are good;
Living His way will let them happen, as they should.

When things go wrong, remember, Satan is on the prowl,
watching, and waiting for you to sin—like a night owl.

Obey the Lord God by doing everything He said,
and you will never die—or WISH you were dead.

Your promised life with God, in the end, will always be,
without Satan or his demons, and FREE from misery!

**Proverbs 4:20-22; John 11:26;
1 Peter 5:8 & Revelation 21:4, 6**

Closing Comments

These poems began after I heard the first rhyming lines in my head! As my awesome Creator prompted me, I wrote down whatever He said!

I pray that your journey in these poems was encouraging, inspiring, and it filled you with hope as you relaxed a while, to focus on the greatness of God.

My genuine desire for you is, you will embrace God's Word with a renewed sense of inspiration, and will be amazed by His lavishing love for you.

When Jesus returns, will He come for you?

To get saved today, go to the Prayer of Salvation on page 129 and sincerely pray. Congratulations to each person who repents and receives Jesus. Tell someone about this decision and find a local church that preaches that Jesus is the **only** way to God!

Candice

God Loves...You!

**The picture below is a thought-provoking display
of God's love for...you!**

**Do you understand the reason Jesus died was so God
could forgive the sins of everyone who believes
in Jesus and give eternal life to them?**